PECANS

PECANS

RECIPES & HISTORY OF AN AMERICAN NUT

BARBARA BRYANT & BETSY FENTRESS

RECIPES BY REBECCA LANG

PHOTOGRAPHS BY ROBERT HOLMES

WITH CONTRIBUTIONS FROM CELEBRATED CHEFS AND FOOD WRITERS

RIZZOLI
NEW YORK

New York · Paris · London · Milan

First published in the United States in 2019 by
Rizzoli International Publications, Inc.
300 Park Avenue South
New York, NY 10010
www.rizzoliusa.com

Recipes: Rebecca Lang
Photography: Robert Holmes

Publisher: Charles Miers
Design and Production: Jennifer Barry Design, Fairfax, CA
Production Assistance: Shelly Peppel
Illustration on page 1: Maryjo Koch
Illustration on page 160: *Pecan Varieties*, by Deborah G. Passmore, 1904;
     Special Collections, USDA Agricultural Library
Additional photography: Andrea Johnson and Jennifer Barry
Food Styling: Kim Kissling
Production Manager: Colin Hough-Trapp
Editorial Coordination: Jono Jarrett
Managing Editor: Lynn Scrabis

Printed in China

2020 2021 2022 2023 / 10 9 8 7 6 5 4 3 2

ISBN: 978-0-8478-6456-0
Library of Congress Control Number: 2019931787

Visit us online:
Facebook.com/RizzoliNewYork
Twitter: @Rizzoli_Books
Instagram.com/RizzoliBooks
Pinterest.com/RizzoliBooks
Youtube.com/user/RizzoliNY
Issuu.com/Rizzoli

CONTENTS

PREFACE

I love pecans. Fresh. Roasted. Chopped. Whole. For as long as I can remember, pecans have been a part of our family kitchen. My mother didn't enjoy cooking, but she did it anyway, and our family of seven thrived on her nutritious meals. Everything tasted better with pecans, according to her, so I grew up loving them—not because she told me to but because she was right. My favorite memory of my mother's cooking is her pecan waffles—the perfect marriage of flavor and crispiness. Hers were smothered in *real* maple syrup and mine with homemade jam, a squeeze of lemon, or nothing at all. As the waffles sizzled on the griddle, the whole kitchen smelled heavenly.

Most people have pecan memories, many of them centered on holiday celebrations. A treasured part of our Thanksgiving and Christmas was oven-roasted pecans coated with lots of butter and a generous sprinkling of salt. We called this delicious cocktail snack Funsten pecans, after my precious aunt Georgeanne Funsten. Her family was in the pecan business for many years, and she made sure we had plenty of pecans year-round. Pecans, almonds, and walnuts—all in the shell—were always stuffed into the toe of our Christmas stockings, along with a navel orange. Where were the little chocolate soldiers my friends got? Fresh nuts were a delicacy I did not appreciate then, but I do now.

But nuts are more than a holiday treat or topping. Their historical importance in agriculture, trade, culture, art, and in the lives of indigenous peoples is fascinating reading. Our cookbook *Almonds: Recipes, History, Culture*, told the history of the almond dating back to the time of the Silk Road. In contrast, the pecan is our North American native nut whose longevity would not have been possible without our diverse culture. We have the Native Americans to thank for discovering and planting pecans across the South and Southwest, and we have an African American slave and gardener to thank for his experimentation with pecan rootstock to graft the successful Centennial tree that made the pecan the popular nut it is today. In *Pecans: Recipes & History of a Native American Nut*, we share with you history, recipes, and chefs' stories that attest to the glory of this extraordinary nut. How marvelous that something so small can bring so much pleasure. We hope you enjoy celebrating this culinary and historical treasure with us.

—BARBARA BRYANT

INTRODUCTION

As the only major nut tree indigenous to North America, the pecan holds a special place in our country's cuisine. Rich in nutrients, steeped in history, and a favorite delicacy of presidents and native peoples, pecans are one of the true heritage foods of the United States.

AMERICA'S PECAN: BEGINNINGS

The migration routes and cultivation of the pecan by Native Americans, presidents, botanists, and African American slaves make for a compelling read. To explore the history of how pecans have come to be so prominent on plates around the world is endlessly fascinating and worth every forkful.

A close relative of the hickory, pecan trees were growing wild in America long before the Europeans arrived. The first trees were found along the Mississippi River and west into Texas, and as far north as Indiana and Kansas. Pecans flourished and spread throughout the Southeast and Southwest. Named after an Algonquian phrase meaning "taking a stone to crack," the pecan became invaluable to Native Americans.

Migration was the key factor in the spread of pecan trees. Native Americans in southern Mississippi are thought to have been some of the first people to add the pecan to their diet. They used broken limbs or long sticks to shake and knock the nuts onto the ground for gathering, a primitive invention that, though now mechanized, is not much different from methods used today. We do know that the pecan harvest determined migration routes, and early Native American tribes depended on pecans for about four months of the year.

As they traveled the Mississippi River and its many tributaries, the tribes carried this compact food, finding myriad uses for it—as nourishment, as medicine, and certainly as barter. Pecan leaves were dried and ground to cure ringworm, while the bark was boiled down in a decoction to treat tuberculosis and used to make tea to soothe upset stomachs. Fermented pecan powder became what is thought to have been the first nut milk.

Native Americans gathering and grinding nuts; painting by Greg Harlin; McClung Museum of Natural History and Culture, University of Tennessee, Knoxville. 2001.8.2

In its role as currency, the pecan was extremely valuable in tribal trading, even more so than freshwater pearls. This bartering of the cherished nut ensured its continued proliferation, as tribes traveled across the immediate region and beyond.

Early French and Spanish explorers encountered pecan trees and admired their fruits enough to make note of the delicate, fine-flavored nuts in their journals and travel accounts. In 1528, a group of almost three hundred Spanish explorers were on a North American mission that went terribly wrong. Four years later, only four survivors remained. One of them, Álvar Núñez Cabeza de Vaca, wrote the first record of the pecan in his journal. He lived among the Quevene, Yguase, and Mariame tribes along the Guadalupe River in Texas, known to the Indians as "the river of nuts" because it was shaded entirely by thriving pecan trees.

Native Americans may have led the charge in expanding the growing region of the pecan, but some members of the animal kingdom contributed as well. Squirrels and small mammals spread the nuts as they foraged and buried stockpiles for winter, while crows flying with pecans would drop the nuts, playing a small role in the proliferation of the trees.

THE RISE OF PECAN SEEDLINGS

Inevitably, pecans spread beyond Texas and the Mississippi River lowlands, attracting devotion and attention both in the Northeast and abroad. Renowned botanist John Bartram, a resident of Philadelphia, friend of Benjamin Franklin, and often called "the father of American botany," first collected pecans in Ohio in 1761 and mailed them to a friend in England. They are believed to be the first pecans to arrive in the British Isles. In the mid-1770s, William Bartram, John Bartram's son and a noted explorer in the Southeast, declared the pecan "one of the most useful trees of the country."

British botanist Thomas Walter settled in Charleston, South Carolina, in the mid-eighteenth century, where he became enamored of the variety of local plants. In *Flora Caroliniana*, a comprehensive volume on the region's flowering plants published in 1788, he noted the details of the pecan tree's leaves but also that he hadn't seen any fruit borne.

Farther north, in Flushing, New York, Prince Nursery was growing pecan trees

William Bartram, by Charles Willson Peale; courtesy Independence National Historical Park

West front of Monticello and garden, depicting Thomas Jefferson's grandchildren, 1825, watercolor by Jane Braddick Peticolas; Alamy Photo

commercially by 1772. After planting thirty nuts, ten pecan trees grew, eight of which were sold to customers in England. As appreciation for pecans grew, so did demand for them. George Washington first fell for the pecan while serving in the army during the Revolutionary War. It was noted by a Frenchman serving alongside him that Washington kept pecans in his pockets and was "constantly eating them." After Washington settled at Mount Vernon, records show that he planted the first pecan trees there in 1775.

Another founding father, Thomas Jefferson, also favored the pecan. While serving as the ambassador to France, he wrote to a friend in Philadelphia asking that he be sent fresh pecans, relying on John Bartram to recommend the best shipping method. Following his time in France, Jefferson set out to grow his own pecans at his home at Monticello. He often wrote to ask friends and family in pecan-growing areas to send him fresh pecans to tide him over until he could harvest his own. Around 1790, Jefferson planted two hundred pecan nuts at Monticello over a five-year span. He is believed to have been the first to grow the trees as an orchard, and recorded historical notes about pecans in his garden journals. The pecan trees were removed in 2004 to preserve the historic home.

Former President Barack Obama's snack of choice was almonds, but founding father George Washington preferred pecans. According to a soldier who served in Washington's army and was the brother of French botanist Georges Louis Marie DuMont de Courset, the commander was forever munching on pecans and always had some in his pocket. An early enthusiast of the pecan, Washington's written records show that he received pecan nuts from Philadelphia and planted them in March 1775 at his historic Virginia estate, Mount Vernon. According to *A List of Ornamental Trees and Shrubs Noted in the Writings and Diaries of George Washington*, the first US president then planted more pecans, or "Illinois nuts" as they were sometimes called, in May 1786. Later, while in Philadelphia, Washington sent nuts for planting in his botanical garden at Mount Vernon in 1787, and again in 1794 and 1795. Washington's love of pecans was shared by another founding father, Thomas Jefferson, who, at Washington's request, sent a quantity of pecan nuts to Washington in the mid-1790s.

Until the mid-2010s, the oldest known pecan tree at Mount Vernon, which stood 145 feet (44 m) tall and weighed an estimated 50 tons (45,360 kg), was situated near the southeast corner of the mansion near Washington's bedroom and office. It had been planted sometime in the 1860s, a little more than sixty years after his death. In 2013, the caretakers of Mount Vernon faced a difficult decision about the approximately 154-year-old tree, the growth of which was gradually threatening to damage the mansion. To avoid any harm to the centerpiece of Washington's estate, the tree was removed in 2014. —BLAKE HALLANAN, *journalist*

Mount Vernon's 154-year-old pecan tree before its removal in 2014, photograph © Kevin Ambrose

Young Virginian, photograph of exhibition diorama of George Washington as a young surveyor in Virginia, c. 1752, courtesy of Mount Vernon Ladies' Association

THE CULTIVATED PECAN

If you planted one hundred pecans and nurtured them into nut-bearing mature trees, every single tree would be a unique variety. That means that grafting is essential to ensuring the uniform nuts required for successful commercial production. Grafting, the method most commonly used today, involves a limb with buds being united to an established rootstock.

Dr. Abner Landrum from South Carolina mastered the budding of pecans around 1822, but his pecan propagation method didn't catch on because no viable nurseries were nearby for sales. It was a slave named Antoine on a sugarcane plantation in Louisiana that successfully grafted pecan trees and forever altered the crop. Jacques Télésphore Roman, the owner of Oak Alley Plantation, was given graft wood from a neighbor who had a tree that produced large, thin-shelled pecans. Roman worked at grafting techniques but was unsuccessful. He turned to Antoine, his talented slave gardener, for help (unfortunately, only Antoine's first name was recorded). In 1846, Antoine successfully grafted 16 trees and then ultimately grafted a total of 126 pecan trees at Oak Alley. By the end of the Civil War in 1865, Antoine's grafted trees were bearing nuts.

Pecans continued their ascent in America's history, when, in 1876, Philadelphia hosted the Centennial Exposition in honor of the one hundredth anniversary of the Declaration of Independence. Over ten million visitors attended this first world's fair held in the United States. Innovations such as Heinz ketchup, Alexander Graham Bell's telephone, and even an arm of the much-anticipated Statue of Liberty were on display. Hubert Bonzano, the new owner at Oak Valley, applied to display nuts from the trees originally grafted by Antoine. Amid the awards and accolades, Antoine's botanical handiwork was named "Centennial" and became the earliest recognized pecan variety. It then went on to become the first pecan variety planted in orchards for the sole purpose of producing pecans commercially.

Today, the United States Department of Agriculture (USDA) and extension agents are industry leaders in breeding and cultivating pecans as a commercial crop. First known as the Bureau of Plant Industry, the USDA began a pecan breeding program in 1930 in Brownsville, Texas. Now with a location in College Station, Texas, as well, the breeding program is home to the largest collection of pecan cultivars in the world, numbering over 250, and to the world's largest collection of pecan nuts.

African American slave on a southern plantation in the 1800s. © Culture Club / Getty Images

The correct way to say the word *pecan* is debated nearly as much as the proper way to make a pecan pie. There is no right or wrong way to pronounce it, thank goodness! The fairly short word can sound drastically different, however, depending on where you were raised.

Pee-KAHN is the most common pronunciation across most of America. Follow along the Eastern Seaboard through the South and even into the extreme Northeast and you'll find PEE-can. Near the Great Lakes, PEE-kahn is standard, while Peh-KAHN can be heard from the Mississippi River west to Texas and Oklahoma. In some pockets of the South, peh-CAN is common. Sometimes even how the word is used determines the pronunciation. Referring to the nut may be peh-KAHN, but when talking about the pie, it's PEE-can.

The Roots of Pecan

It's not a coincidence that pecan trees have become deeply embedded in the very culture of the states where they grow. In the early 1900s, real estate developers planted pecan trees in Georgia as part of marketing land to new residents. These "pecan plantations" in the western part of the state could draw a higher price, which translated into higher demand.

On a practical level, as pecans took hold in the Deep South in the early twentieth century, the shade offered by the trees provided much-appreciated respite from the punishing sun. With no air-conditioning and extreme heat and humidity, southerners took advantage of the pecan trees' large canopies and tall crowns in the summer, as well as the nuts that collected on the ground in the fall.

Pecans are almost omnipresent in southern cooking, and nowadays are even used in craft beer brewing and for pecan-infused whiskey. Pralines appear to have been brought to New Orleans by French Ursuline nuns in 1727. Eventually, the native Louisiana pecan was substituted for the almond, and became a staple sweet in New Orleans. In the 1880s, the first pecan pie recipe appeared, but bragging rights about where it originated vary, with Texas, Nashville, and St. Louis all claiming to be home to the first published recipe. By the end of the nineteenth century, pecan recipes were appearing regularly in American cookbooks.

As pecans grew more common in the cuisines of the Deep South and of neighboring Texas, they also became part of the identity of many states. Texas has over seventy streams named in honor of the pecan, and in 1919, the pecan became the state tree. The love of pecans in Texas started over a century ago, when Governor James Stephen Hogg asked his family to skip a gravestone and instead, "Let my children plant at the head of my grave a pecan tree and at my feet an old-fashioned walnut tree. And when these trees shall bear, let the pecans and the walnuts be given out among the plain people so that they may plant them and make Texas a land of trees."

Pecans have also influenced state nomenclature. Drive into the town of Pecan, Mississippi, and you'll soon find the Pecan Post Office. Louisiana is home to the Pecan Landing Oil Field and Pecan Island. In 1982, the pecan officially became the state nut of Alabama. No matter the state, as long as pecans are growing, they make an impact that goes beyond their role as a commodity crop. They have shaped agriculture, cuisine, and commerce and continue to be a staple in the lives of those who live around them.

The pecan is memorialized by a giant statue in Seguin, Texas.

THE ORCHARD

If you haven't seen a pecan orchard, it's hard to imagine the fanned-out limbs reaching for sunshine while simultaneously creating a canopy that shades everything beneath them. Pecan orchards are also places where not only pecans are plentiful but also where peaches, clover, grazing cows, or picnicking admirers can be found.

With the discovery of improved pecan varieties, orchards began to be planted by growers throughout the South and Southwest in hopes of reaping great benefits. Native seed-lings can produce as much as 700 pounds (320 kg) of pecans per acre (0.4 ha), while improved varieties can yield almost twice that amount. Orchards of improved varieties account for 85 percent of US pecan production.

Many pecan growers choose carefully what grows under their trees to make the most of their orchard space. Cattle grazing under the shade of pecan trees are a benefit to the trees—thanks to the natural nitrogen the cows leave behind—as long as they are moved away from the orchards well before it's time for harvest so they don't trample the nuts.

Rye, hairy vetch, and several species of clover are popular to plant as winter cover crops (crops grown on the orchard floor primarily to improve soil health) to supply nitrogen and for erosion control. Planting legumes is beneficial, too, as they both reseed themselves and add nitrogen. Sufficient nitrogen can be furnished to the soil through such crops alone, but phosphorus, calcium, and potassium are normally added through the use of fertilizers.

The economics of growing pecans is made much more sustainable by intercropping the orchards (growing other crops alongside the pecan trees) in the early years, as it takes nearly a decade for an orchard to yield fruit. Once pecan trees are producing nuts, intercropping is no longer recommended. For example, peach trees and pecan trees can be planted at the same time. The peach trees are ready for harvest in two years, whereas the pecan trees will need another eight to ten years before they begin producing. That means the grower can utilize the peaches while waiting on the first nut harvest. Peach trees also have much shorter lives, sometimes even aging out before pecans are in full production. Early vegetables (harvested in the first weeks of summer) can also provide an income while waiting on the first harvest of pecans. Corn and cowpeas, for example, have proven to work as successful intercrops. Cotton is another good candidate for intercropping.

PECAN PRODUCTION AND EXPORTATION

Georgia, Texas, and New Mexico are the three largest pecan-producing states. Their orchards—depending on humidity and water sources—are vastly different in appearance. In New Mexico, orchards require more irrigation than those planted farther east, and the orchard floors are less lush, often with no groundcover. But the lower humidity is a great benefit to the health of the Southwest groves.

Left: Young pecan trees are cultivated in neatly planted rows at Jeffreys Ranch Pecans in California. Above: A Texas orchard (left) is aided by beneficial cover crops. Nuts are harvested with the aid of a mechanical shaker (right) at Pearson Farm, a fifth generation grower that also culitvates peaches in Fort Valley, Georgia.

WORLD PECAN PRODUCTION

The United States produces 80 percent of the world's pecans with an annual crop of about 300 million pounds (136,077,000 kg) from more than ten million trees. Mexico ranks second in production with 222 million pounds (100,700,000 kg). Other countries that produce pecans commercially include Australia, Brazil, Israel, Peru, and South Africa.

Georgia, Texas, and New Mexico account for over three-fourths of the pecan production in the US, with twelve other states in the South, Southwest, and West making up the remainder of the production. The annual domestic consumption and foreign exports are as follows:

U.S. Domestic Use	45%
China	28%
Mexico	15%
Canada	5%
Netherlands	3%
United Kingdom	2%
Others	2%

Orchards occasionally have to be thinned or older trees replaced with new ones. Rarely would pecan trees be grown only for timber, so any trees that are cut are put to good use. As one of the hardest and strongest woods available, pecan is often used where shock resistance or strength is necessary, such as for baseball bats, ladder rungs, and wheel spokes. Small trees and untreated remnants can be chipped and used for smoking meats on a grill.

America grew from a frontier of unspoiled lands with wild pecan trees into a country that now grows over 80 percent of the world's total pecan crop. As early as 1840, American pecans were being shipped to Europe for sale. The exportation of US pecans gained steam as the number of orchards and their productivity grew.

Today, China is the largest importer of American pecans, followed by, in order, the European Union, Vietnam, Saudi Arabia, Kuwait, India, Turkey, and South Korea. Unlike many edibles, once their moisture has dropped to below 5 percent, the nuts can be shipped in nonrefrigerated containers. The states engaged in commercial pecan production are Alabama, Arkansas, Arizona, California, Florida, Georgia, Kansas, Louisiana, Missouri, Mississippi, North Carolina, New Mexico, Oklahoma, South Carolina, and Texas.

STAPLE AT HOME, DELICACY ABROAD

American pecan growers took an active role in championing the pecan to China when China joined the World Trade Organization in 2001. The Chinese were already big fans of the hickory nut, and it didn't take long for their hunger for pecans to grow. Today, more than one-third of the US pecan crop is exported to China.

The Chinese lightly crack the shells, bathe the nuts in flavored water, and then dry roast them for a snack known as *bi gen guo*. Especially prevalent around Chinese New Year, *bi gen guo* are sold in a number of flavors, with vanilla the most popular. The demand in China is so high that new acreage in the United States is being devoted to grafted, improved trees to ensure production of the thin-shelled, large, more uniform nuts the Chinese prefer.

Above: Fifth generation Texas pecan growers Kristin and Winston Millican inspect a grove of older pecan trees in their family's 130-year-old orchard in San Saba. Mature trees can grow over 130 feet (40 m) tall with a spread as wide as 75 feet (23 m). Far left: Father and son, Bob (right) and Winston Millican, of the Millican Pecan Company, show off their harvest.

CULTIVATION ON THE FARM

Although there are about one hundred pecan varieties, only about thirty are used for commercial harvesting. Cultivating pecans requires a science that blends weather, natural forces, and farming techniques, and irrigation is used almost universally to supplement rainfall. The USDA and extension agents have been invaluable to farmers in learning best practices for implementing ongoing research and technology advancement to produce pest-resistant trees.

Late fall, after harvest, the pecan leaves are killed by the first freeze, and the tree enters into a dormant period. Between March and May, fertilization occurs and new leaves follow. Each leaf can be as long as 20 inches (50 cm) and has nine to

Above: Jeffreys Ranch Pecans is a fifth generation farm in northern California.
Right: The San Saba River runs through pecan country in central Texas, providing natural irrigation to dozens of farms along its banks.

seventeen serrated leaflets. When pecans in large orchards are ready for harvesting and shelling, farm equipment is preset to the dimensions of the nuts. This is yet another reason why improved grafted pecans are necessary, as harvesting is much more efficient when all of the nuts are of uniform size.

There are over five hundred cultivars of improved varieties. Stuart, Schley, Caddo, Desirable, Moreland, and Cape Fear are among the most popular. It's very difficult for a nonprofessional to identify the variety based on the appearance of the tree alone, however. The best way to identify them is at harvest, when the pecans are at full maturation.

PESTICIDES, DISEASES, AND THEIR REMEDIES

Pecan growers must be vigilant in the battle to keep their orchards healthy and productive. The pests that like pecans are plentiful, and determined. Mistletoe can invade and infect trees until the grower intervenes. A spray can eradicate the mistletoe, and then the limb is pruned, or the mistletoe itself is cut out of the tree. Other enemies are rosette and mouse-ear plants and the pecan scab fungus. Extension agents are essential in learning about new pests and diseases and the way to treat them. The health of pecan trees becomes a bit of a community effort among agents and growers.

Harvesting and Shelling

In pecan country, the first few pecans hitting the ground are something of a ceremonial beginning to fall. Dry weather is essential for a successful harvest. If the pecans drop onto wet soil and are allowed to remain there too long, the tannins in the shells can leach into the nuts, imparting a bitter flavor.

The fresher the pecan, the more delicate the flavor and the more desirable the nut in the marketplace. Because fresh pecans are highly sensitive to moisture, the nuts are promptly dried to a point of 8 percent moisture (which eventually drops to 5 percent or lower) during processing. Pecans right off the tree also have more butter-like flavor than ones purchased later in the season. That buttery quality is due to their high fat content (around 70 percent), which means the nuts can become rancid if processing is slowed.

After the nuts are harvested from the ground, they must first be separated from any "bycatch," such as small rocks and sticks inadvertently picked up along with the nuts. The freshly harvested nuts are then sometimes polished to remove any dark streaks on the shells, a step that is strictly cosmetic. Next, they are sanitized and sent into the crackers, which loosen the shells from the nutmeats. Finally, the sheller knocks off the shells, leaving just the nutmeats, which are sorted by size before packaging.

Left: (top to bottom) Pecans are harvested from mid-October to the end of November in the Northern Hemisphere. A harvesting shaker rolls through a Texas pecan grove as harvest begins. A tractor transports the harvest at Nilo Plantation in Albany, Georgia to a shelling facility. Recently harvested pecans at Millican Pecan Company are first shelled and then sorted by size and quality.
Right: Clusters of pecan flowers, called catkins, bloom in spring.

Pollination in the pecan orchard is critical to both the yield and the quality of the nuts. To produce nuts successfully, pecan trees must be cross-pollinated. April and May are the season of pollination, and the trees are pollinated by wind, rather than by such better-known pollinators as bees. When planting orchards, many growers keep this in mind to determine the proper spacing of the trees.

Pecan trees are monoecious, which means both the male and female flowers are on the same tree. Female flower pistils are located at the end of the current season's growth, and the male flowers, called catkins, are located at the end of the last season's growth. Catkins look like thin, golden tassels and are easy to spot dangling from trees during the early spring. An average bearing tree is likely to produce several thousand of these colorful tassels, and a single catkin can produce enough pollen to pollinate flowers that may yield up to 50,000 pounds (22,700 kg) of average-size pecans.

NUTRIENT-RICH PECANS

Nuts rank among the most protein rich and nutrient dense of any plant-based food. The world's five longest-lived cultures, known as The Blue Zones, all strongly emphasize nuts as a staple food in their diet.

In 2013, researchers at the Harvard School of Public Health published a study that found that people who ate nuts every day lived longer, healthier lives than those who did not consume nuts at all. The study also concluded that those who ate the most nuts—seven or more servings per week—were at a greater advantage to live significantly longer, disease-free lives, even considering other lifestyle factors.

Pecans, in particular, are an excellent source of the minerals magnesium, manganese, copper, and thiamine. Among other longevity benefits, these nutrients are known for their ability to improve and maintain peak brain function throughout a person's life. Studies also reveal a beneficial spike in the brainwave frequencies associated with overall cognition, learning, memory, and healing when pecans are consumed often.

—ELIZABETH HOWES, MS,
functional wellness strategist, chef, and
author of *The Modern Salad*

CREATIVE REUSE OF PECAN SHELLS

Pecan shellers rarely dispose of shells, as they are a profitable commodity with a variety of uses. Crushed shells can be used as mulch in landscaping and to provide acidity to garden soil, and like pecan wood, they can be added to backyard grills for a sublime, smoky flavor. The inner lining of pecan shells yields tannins used in tanning leather, and ground shells can be mixed with resin to produce a wood-like effect. Pecan shells can even be used to clean jet engines by feeding them through the air intakes! Additionally, finely ground shells, added to soaps and facials scrubs to make an exfoliating cleanser, are a wonderful natural ingredient for homemade beauty products.

NUTRITION

Pecans have been prized for their buttery flavor fresh off the tree for generations, but it's only recently that their incredible nutritional value has been recognized. In 2012, the American Heart Association designated pecans as heart-healthy. According to the Food and Drug Administration, eating 1½ ounces (45 g) of pecans or other nuts each day may reduce the risk of heart disease. Some 90 percent of the fat in pecans is monounsaturated or polyunsaturated, and more than nineteen vitamins and minerals, among them phosphorus, zinc, calcium, folic acid, magnesium, iron, beta-carotene, and vitamins A, B, and E, are packed into every bite. Pecans are also loaded with protein and with naturally occurring antioxidants that may help to decrease the risk of cancer, and they contain no sodium, making them ideal for anyone on a low-sodium diet. Plus, just 1 ounce (30 g) of pecans provides 11 percent of the daily value of fiber.

Right: Pecan shells, tree bark, and leaves are used to make richly colored textile dyes. In Mexico, an artisan weaver grinds the shells into a fine pigment that will be used to dye wool for colorful handwoven rugs.

SHELLS, LEAVES, AND WOOD: USING THE WHOLE PECAN TREE

Before you discard those pecan shells or pecan wood, you may want to consider the host of possibilities for putting them to valuable use. Because of their abundant tannins, neutral flavor, and hardiness, pecan shells, leaves, and wood have a wide range of practical uses, from natural dyes for textiles to garden mulch.

Textile weavers use pecan bark, leaves, or shells to create a dye that is a rich shade of brown. In the garden, the shells and leaves can be used as mulch to help retain moisture in the soil. Because pecan mulch is somewhat acidic, it is especially good for use around azaleas and blueberry bushes.

Pecan wood is highly sought after by woodworkers because of its durability. Its most spectacular use was in 1996, when Georgia pecan wood was selected by the Atlanta Olympic Committee to make the handles of the seventeen thousand torches for the 1996 Olympic Games. The torches were used in the more than 16,000-mile (24,000-km) relay from Greece to Atlanta, Georgia, to light the Olympic flame.

—BLAKE HALLANAN, journalist

Pecans in the Kitchen

It wasn't that many years ago that only those living near a pecan orchard or the owners of a few trees in a backyard would be blessed with pecans in the kitchen. Thankfully, filling up on pecans has become easier than ever. Many large supermarket chains carry pecans in the shell each fall, and even big-box stores sell pecans both shelled and in the shell. Several products that are made with pecans can be used in almost any area of cooking. Pecan flour and meal can be purchased from many online retailers for baking. Substituting them for all-purpose or whole wheat flour is a flavorful gluten-free option for making a wide variety of baked goods and is a terrific source of extra protein.

Creamy pecan butter can be purchased or freshly made from toasted pecans and is a delicious alternative to other nut butters. Pecan oil, pressed from just-harvested pecans, can be used both as a cooking oil and as a finishing oil. Two types are readily available, pecan oil and roasted pecan oil. The oil made from roasted pecans has a much deeper flavor and color and is more expensive, which makes it best for drizzling on finished dishes just before serving. The oil made from raw pecans is very light in flavor and has a high smoke point, making it ideal for all kinds of cooking, from sautéing to panfrying to deep-frying.

Shopping for Pecans

Pecan halves are sold in a number of different sizes: mammoth, extra large, large, medium, small, and midget. Look for nuts that are plump and are a uniform golden honey color. Pieces can also be purchased in a range of sizes. Pecan halves have a longer shelf life than pieces.

Storing Pecans

There are several methods for storing pecans. Choose the best one based on how quickly you will use the nuts and whether or not they are shelled. Shelled pecans should always be stored in an airtight container (alone, so they don't absorb any other food odors). They have a pantry shelf life of about six weeks and will keep in the refrigerator for about nine months or in the freezer for up to two years. They can be thawed and refrozen without compromising flavor. For long-term storage, it's best to leave the nuts in the shell. Unshelled pecans can be stored in an airtight container at room temperature for up to four months or in the freezer for up to four years. Make sure the shells are clean and dry before packing them into a container.

Shelling Pecans

Pecans are usually harvested in one of two ways: they are shaken down (with anything from a weighted cane fishing pole to an industrial machine made expressly for the purpose) or they fall to the ground naturally without any prodding. Once the nuts are on the ground, the clock is ticking. If you're lucky enough to have a pecan tree nearby, gather the nuts from the ground as soon as possible.

Although pecans can be shelled by hand using a variety of hand-powered nutcrackers, southerners have mastered the art of cracking pecans without any type of tool, usually while sitting on the front porch. The favorite method involves nothing more than a hand and a couple of pecans. Hold two pecans in your hand against each other and squeeze. Each will crack with the pressure of the other nut. The hardest part of cracking pecans this way is trying not to eat them immediately!

Toasting Pecans

Toasting shelled pecans brings out their natural oils and intensifies their flavor. To toast chopped pecans, pecan pieces, or pecan halves on the stove top, spread them in a single layer in a dry frying pan and heat over low heat, stirring or shaking the pan occasionally, for 2 to 3 minutes, until they take on color and are fragrant. Watch carefully to prevent burning. Immediately pour the nuts onto a plate to cool.

To toast chopped pecans, pecan pieces, or pecan halves in the oven, spread them in a single layer on a sheet pan and place in a preheated 350°F (180°C) oven for 5 to 7 minutes, until they take on color and are fragrant. Watch carefully to prevent burning. Immediately pour the nuts onto a plate to cool.

Homemade Pecan Staples

Take advantage of harvesttime to create your own fresh pecan products. Making your own pecan butter, meal, and flour at home is remarkably easy. Because pecans have a naturally high oil content, they transform quickly. Pay close attention when grinding pecans in the food processor, as they can go from meal to flour to butter in less than a couple of minutes.

Pecan Meal   Makes 1¾ cups (200 g)

2 cups (200 g) pecan halves, toasted

In a food processor, pulse the pecans about twenty times, until the texture is similar to that of coarse cornmeal. Transfer to an airtight container and store in the freezer for up to 3 months.

Left: (top to bottom) Pecans nuts are most commonly sold in three forms, pieces, halves, and in the shell. Shelled nuts have a shorter storage life than unshelled nuts.
Right: Homemade pecans staples, (top to bottom) flour, meal, and pecan butter

Pecan Flour

MAKES 1²/₃ CUPS (**200** G)

2 cups (200 g) pecan halves, toasted

In a food processor, pulse the pecans about twenty-five times, until the texture is similar to that of fine dried breadcrumbs. It will not be as fine as wheat flour. Transfer to an airtight container and store in the freezer for up to 3 months.

Pecan Butter

MAKES ³/₄ CUP (**233** G)

2 cups (200 g) pecan halves, toasted
Pinch of salt

In a food processor, combine the pecans and salt and process for about 1 minute and 15 seconds, until creamy and spreadable. Transfer to an airtight container and store in the refrigerator for up to 2 weeks. Let sit at room temperature for 10 minutes and stir before using.

Pecan Milk

MAKES ABOUT 5¹/₂ **CUPS (1.3** L)

2 cups (200 g) pecan halves
6 cups (1.5 l) water

Put the pecans in a bowl and add water to cover. Cover the bowl and refrigerate overnight. Drain the pecans in a fine-mesh sieve, over the bowl of a blender. Rinse the nuts under cold running water, and drain again. Add the pecans to the reserved soaking liquid in the blender and process on high speed until liquefied and completely smooth. Strain through the fine-mesh sieve to remove any solid bits. If your sieve isn't fine enough to catch all of the solids, line it with cheesecloth and then strain again. Transfer to an airtight container and flavor to taste with vanilla or other flavoring, if desired. Store chilled for up to 3 days.

BREAKFAST & BREADS

GINGER-PECAN PANCAKES WITH PEAR COMPOTE

Lazy Saturday mornings can still be relaxed when homemade pancakes are sizzling on the griddle. Make the batter up to 2 days in advance and store in the refrigerator. The flavors in the compote get better if you also make it ahead; reheat gently. When cooking pancakes for a crowd, keep each batch warm until serving time in a 175°F (80°C) oven.

COMPOTE

4 red pears, such as Red Anjou
1/2 cup (90 g) golden raisins
1/3 cup (80 ml) fresh orange juice
Juice of 1 lemon
2 tablespoons firmly packed light brown sugar
2 teaspoons chopped fresh rosemary
1/4 teaspoon salt

PANCAKES

2 cups (310 g) all-purpose flour
2 tablespoons granulated sugar
2 1/2 teaspoons baking powder
1 teaspoons baking soda
3/4 teaspoon salt
3/4 teaspoon ground ginger
1/2 teaspoon ground cinnamon
1/4 teaspoon ground allspice
2 large eggs
1 1/2 cups (375 ml) buttermilk
1/2 cup (125 ml) whole milk
4 tablespoons (60 g) unsalted butter, melted
1/2 teaspoon pure vanilla extract
1/2 cup (50 g) pecan halves, toasted and chopped, plus
    more for garnish (optional)

Unsalted butter, for greasing the pan, plus more at room
    temperature, for serving

To make the pear compote, halve and core the unpeeled pears and cut into 1/2-inch (12-mm) pieces. Transfer to a saucepan and add the raisins, orange juice, lemon juice, brown sugar, rosemary, and salt. Place over medium-low heat and cook, stirring every 5 minutes, for about 25 minutes, until pears are soft and liquid is slightly syrupy. Keep warm until serving.

While the compote is cooking, prepare the pancake batter. In a bowl, whisk together the flour, granulated sugar, baking powder, baking soda, salt, ginger, cinnamon, and allspice. In a small bowl, whisk the eggs until blended, then add the buttermilk, milk, butter, and vanilla and whisk until well mixed. Stir the egg mixture into the flour mixture until thoroughly combined. Fold in the pecans.

To cook the pancakes, preheat the oven to 175°F (80°C). Heat a large nonstick frying pan or griddle over medium-low heat and grease lightly with butter. For each pancake, ladle 1/4 cup (60 ml) of the batter onto the hot pan, being careful not to crowd the pancakes. Cook for about 2 minutes, until bubbles form on the surface and the edges look done. Flip and cook for about 3 minutes on the second side, until browned. Transfer to a large heatproof platter and keep warm in the oven. Repeat with the remaining batter.

Serve the pancakes immediately with butter and the compote and garnish with chopped pecans, if desired.

My memories of pecans go back to my childhood, driving across Georgia on the way to Florida and seeing the roadside pecan stands along the way. As a chef, I think of pecans as a southern ingredient, but we're also fortunate to have flavorful local pecans in Missouri. At our restaurant, Louie, we tend to use pecans in desserts and in salads to add crunch, but we also love braising greens and topping them with whole pecans. For a summer menu, we'll strew pecans over a radicchio, green bean, and shallot salad.

A favorite grain salad at the restaurant has pecans as a core ingredient. We cook the nuts until they're nice and toasted; spritz them with water, which causes them to crack; and then sprinkle them with Maldon sea salt. Finally, we chop them with basil, mint, and Sweet 100 tomatoes and toss them with Israeli (pearl) couscous and a light vinaigrette. It's been a favorite dish with our guests for years.

On the sweet side, our house-made granola with pecans gives that final crunch on top of *panna cotta* made with reduced wine–poached rhubarb.

—Matt McGuire, Executive Chef, Louie restaurant, Clayton, Missouri

Pecan Granola with Cherries and Blueberries

MAKES 6 CUPS

Buying packaged granola is unnecessary when a homemade version bursting with sweet and salty flavors is this fast to make. Serve a spoonful over Greek yogurt or as an all-natural cereal with ice-cold milk. For the prettiest presentation, use unsweetened coconut flakes, often called chips, in place of the shredded coconut.

3 cups (270 g) old-fashioned rolled oats
1 cup (90 g) unsweetened shredded dried coconut
1 cup (115 g) chopped pecans
1/3 cup (80 ml) pecan oil
2 tablespoons pure maple syrup
2 tablespoons firmly packed light brown sugar
1/2 teaspoon salt
1 cup (125 g) dried cherries
1 cup (125 g) dried blueberries

Preheat the oven to 350°F (180°C). Line a large sheet pan with parchment paper or aluminum foil.

In a large bowl, combine the oats, coconut, and pecans. In a small bowl, whisk together the oil, maple syrup, sugar, and salt. Pour the oil mixture over the oat mixture and stir until all of the oat mixture is coated with the oil. Turn out onto the prepared pan and spread evenly.

Bake the granola, stirring often, for about 25 minutes, until golden brown. Remove from the oven and let cool for 5 minutes, then stir in the cherries and blueberries. Let cool completely.

Store in an airtight container at room temperature for up to 3 days.

Lemon-Pecan-Pineapple Green Smoothies

You'll be looking forward to sunrise after one taste of this tropical smoothie. It is easy to personalize, too. Add seeds like hemp and chia for crunch or blueberries or avocado for a vitamin boost. Here's a time-saver: Buy a fresh pineapple, peel it and cut it into cubes, freeze the cubes in a single layer on a sheet pan, scoop the frozen cubes into a resealable plastic bag, and return them to the freezer. When you want to make a smoothie, just pop as much of the frozen pineapple as you need into the blender with everything else. This not only saves on prep time but also replaces the need for ice in almost any blended drink.

1-inch (2.5-cm) piece fresh ginger, peeled and chopped
1/2 cup (50 g) pecan halves, toasted
2 tablespoons fresh lemon juice
4 cups (625 g) chopped fresh pineapple
1 1/2 cups (97 g) stemmed and chopped kale
2/3 cup (170 g) plain whole-milk Greek yogurt
1/4 cup (60 ml) coconut milk

In a blender, combine the ginger, pecans, and lemon juice and pulse until the nuts are finely ground. Add the pineapple, kale, yogurt, and coconut milk and blend until completely smooth. Serve immediately.

PECAN-FLAVORED BUTTERS

Sweet butter combined with pecans is an added luxury on almost anything from fresh breads to grilled steaks. Store these butters in airtight containers or rolled into sliceable logs and wrapped well in parchment paper. They will keep in the refrigerator for up to 2 weeks.

HONEY PECAN BUTTER   MAKES ½ CUP (125 g)

½ cup (125g) unsalted butter, at room temperature
2 tablespoons finely chopped toasted pecans
⅛ teaspoon ground cinnamon
1 tablespoon honey
Pinch of salt

In a small bowl, combine all of the ingredients and mix well.

PEACH PECAN BUTTER   MAKES ¾ CUP (185 g)

½ cup (125 g) unsalted butter, at room temperature
3 tablespoons finely chopped toasted pecans
2 tablespoons peach preserves
1 teaspoon finely chopped fresh rosemary
Pinch of salt

In a small bowl, combine all of the ingredients and mix well.

CHILE-PECAN-LIME BUTTER   MAKES ¾ CUP (185 g)

½ cup (125 g) unsalted butter, at room temperature
¼ fresh red chile, finely diced
Finely grated zest of 1 lime
3 tablespoons finely chopped toasted pecans
Pinch of salt

In a small bowl, combine all of the ingredients and mix well.

PECAN, BROWN SUGAR, AND SAGE CRUSTED BACON Serves 6 to 8

Just when you thought you couldn't love bacon more, smothering each slice with a slather of tangy, sweet-and-spicy topping turns a standard breakfast side into an addicting one. If you prefer a little heat, add 1/8 teaspoon cayenne pepper to the brown sugar mixture. The bacon drippings and the sugar will cause some smoke in the oven, but you will forget all about it the moment you taste the result. The sweet and savory slices are just as good at room temperature as they are warm straight from the oven.

Nonstick cooking spray, for the sheet pan
1/2 cup (58 g) very finely chopped pecans
1/2 cup (105 g) firmly packed light brown sugar
1 1/2 tablespoons balsamic vinegar
1 tablespoon very finely chopped fresh sage
1 teaspoon freshly ground black pepper
1 package (1 pound/500 g) sliced bacon (not thick-cut)

Still Life with Fruit and Nuts, 1848, painting by Robert Seldon Duncanson, National Gallery of Art

Preheat the oven to 400°F (200°C). Line a large sheet pan with aluminum foil. Set an ovenproof wire rack over the foil, then lightly spray the rack with cooking spray.

In a small bowl, stir together the pecans, brown sugar, vinegar, sage, and pepper. Arrange the bacon slices in a single layer on the prepared rack. Spread the bacon generously with the sugar-pecan mixture (about 1 tablespoon per slice).

Bake for 25 to 30 minutes, until the bacon is slightly crispy or until cooked as desired.

Muffins Loaded with Oats, Pecans, Pineapple, and Dates

Combining pecans, oats, and whole wheat flour with sweet pineapple and dates makes a batter that bakes into muffins filling enough to be breakfast all by themselves. Just one of these hearty gems will fortify you all the way to lunch, so they are perfect for busy mornings, whether off to school or work. Bake a batch and store them in an airtight container at room temperature for up to 2 days or in the freezer for up to 1 month.

1 cup (155 g) whole wheat flour

1/2 cup (45 g) old-fashioned rolled oats

1 teaspoon salt

1 teaspoon baking soda

1 teaspoon baking powder

1/2 teaspoon ground cinnamon

3/4 cup (180 ml) vegetable oil

2 large eggs

1 can (8 ounces/250 g) crushed pineapple in 100 percent juice, undrained

1/2 cup (105 g) firmly packed light brown sugar

11/2 teaspoons pure vanilla extract

Finely grated zest of 1 lemon

1/2 cup (90 g) chopped dates

1/2 cup (58 g) chopped pecans, toasted

Preheat the oven to 400°F (200°C). Line 18 muffin cups with paper liners.

In a bowl, stir together the flour, oats, salt, baking soda, baking powder, and cinnamon. In a stand mixer fitted with the paddle attachment, combine the oil, eggs, and pineapple and beat on low speed until blended. Add the sugar, vanilla, and lemon zest and beat on low speed for about 1 minute, until well mixed.

On low speed, slowly add the flour mixture to the oil mixture, stopping the mixer once to scrape down the sides of the bowl, until incorporated. Fold in the dates and pecans just until evenly distributed. Spoon the batter into the prepared muffin cups, filling each one about two-thirds full.

Bake the muffins for 16 to 17 minutes, until browned and a toothpick inserted into the center of a muffin comes out clean with a few moist crumbs attached. Let cool on a wire rack for about 20 minutes, then turn the muffins out onto the rack. Serve warm or at room temperature.

BUTTERMILK PECAN BISCUITS

Buttermilk is just one way to make a biscuit better—and pecans are another! Adding toasted pecans gives these featherlight biscuits a buttery crunch. Be sure to use self-rising soft-wheat flour—the secret to fluffy southern biscuits. Although it seems a natural motion, don't be tempted to twist the biscuit cutter. Just the slightest rotation can turn out an uneven (called lopsided in the South) biscuit. For a heartier, meal-in-one variation, split the hot biscuits and stuff with thinly sliced cooked country ham. About 1/4 pound (125 g) ham is all you will need.

1 1/2 cups (210 g) self-rising soft-wheat flour
(such as White Lily), plus more for the work surface
and 1 cup (140 g) for kneading

4 tablespoons (60 g) unsalted butter, cut into small pieces

2/3 cup (160 ml) buttermilk

1/4 cup (60 ml) heavy cream

1/2 cup (50 g) pecan halves, toasted and finely chopped

Preheat the oven to 425°F (220°C). Have ready a large light-colored sheet pan.

Put the 1 1/2 cups (210 g) flour into a large bowl and scatter the butter over the top. Using a pastry blender or two knives, cut the butter into the flour until the butter is thoroughly distributed and the mixture forms large, coarse crumbs. Add the buttermilk, cream, and pecans and stir just until the mixture holds together and begins to pull away from the sides of the bowl as the dough begins to form. Do not overmix, to prevent tough biscuits from forming.

Dust a work surface generously with flour and turn the dough out onto it. Using floured hands, knead the dough, folding it over on itself and pressing down with the heels of your hands, four or five times, gradually adding as much of the remaining 1 cup (140 g) flour as needed to make a dough that clings together and is not sticky.

With a light touch, pat the dough into a round about 3/4 inch (2 cm) thick. Using a 2-inch (5-cm) round biscuit cutter, and cutting straight down and pulling straight up, cut out as many rounds as possible and transfer them to the ungreased sheet pan, spacing them about 1 inch (2.5 cm) apart. Gather together the dough scraps, pat into a round about 3/4 inch (2 cm) thick, cut out as many rounds as possible, and add them to the sheet pan. Discard any remaining scraps.

Bake for 18 to 19 minutes, until lightly browned. Remove from the oven, let cool slightly on the pan on a wire rack, and serve warm with butter and honey or your favorite jam.

RUSTIC PECAN FLOUR YEAST BREAD

Consider making this simple, everyday bread a staple in your kitchen, especially for morning toast. Add wheat germ, bran, toasted chia or sunflower seeds, or even chopped pecans for extra texture and nutrition. Try it the next day sliced, toasted, and spread with honey or with a sweet pecan butter (page 44).

4 cups (630 g) bread flour, plus more for the work surface
1 cup (120 g) pecan flour (page 33)
2½ teaspoons salt
1½ cups (375 ml) warm water (105° to 115°F/40° to 46°C)
3 tablespoons honey
1 package (2¼ teaspoons/7 g) active dry yeast
Vegetable oil, for oiling the bowl and pans

In a large bowl, whisk together the bread flour, pecan flour, and salt. In a small bowl, stir together the warm water, honey, and yeast and let stand 5 to 10 minutes. The surface will become slightly foamy. Make a well in the center of the flour mixture. Pour the yeast mixture into the well and stir with a wooden spoon just until the flour mixture is moistened and forms a rough mass.

Dust a work surface with bread flour and turn the dough out onto it. Knead the dough, folding it over on itself and pressing down with the heels of your hands, for about 5 minutes, until smooth and elastic. Shape the dough into a ball. Oil a large bowl, transfer the dough to the bowl, and turn the dough once to coat it with oil. Cover the bowl with a damp kitchen towel or plastic wrap and let the dough rise in a warm place (85°F/30°C) for 1½ to 2 hours, until doubled in volume.

Grease two 4½-by-8½-by-2½-inch (11.5-by-21.5-by-6-cm) loaf pans with oil. Dust a work surface with flour, then punch down the dough and transfer it to the floured surface. Divide the dough in half. Gently flatten half of the dough into a rough rectangle. Starting from one end, fold one-third of the dough over on itself, then fold the other end over the doubled thirds, overlapping them. Pinch all of the seams closed. The dough should be taut. Place the loaf, seam side down, into a prepared pan. Repeat with the remaining dough and transfer to the second pan. Cover the pans with a dry kitchen towel and let the dough rise in a warm place for about 45 minutes, until doubled in volume. After about 25 minutes, preheat the oven to 425°F (220°C).

Bake the bread for 15 minutes. Lower the oven temperature to 375°F (190°C) and continue to bake for 15 to 20 minutes longer, until golden brown on top and the bottom sounds hollow when tapped with your fingers. Let cool in the pans on wire racks for 5 minutes, then turn the loaves out of the pans, right side up, and let cool completely before serving.

The loaves can be tightly wrapped and stored at room temperature for up to 2 days or in the freezer for up to 1 month.

Pecan-Raisin Cinnamon Roll Pull-Apart Bread   Makes 2 loaves

*All the comforting goodness of a warm cinnamon roll is packed into
a loaf pan for an easy morning sweet treat. Serving the bread
doesn't even require a knife. Simply pull off the irresistible glazed and
sugared sections. Make the loaf the night before serving and refrigerate
after the second rise. Let the dough sit at room temperature for
30 minutes, then bake as directed.*

1 cup (250 ml) whole milk

1/2 cup (125 g) unsalted butter, plus 6 tablespoons (90 g),
    melted

1/4 cup (50 g) granulated sugar

1 teaspoon salt

1 package (2 1/4 teaspoons/7 g) active dry yeast

3 1/2 cups (540 g) all-purpose flour, plus more for
    the work surface

3 tablespoons granulated sugar

1 teaspoon ground cinnamon

1 cup (100 g) pecan halves, chopped

1 cup (185 g) golden raisins

Icing

1 cup (125 g) powdered sugar

2 tablespoons whole milk

In a saucepan, combine the milk, 1/2 cup (125 g) butter, sugar,
and salt, set over medium-low heat, and stir until the butter
melts. Let stand for about 20 minutes, until cooled to 105 to
115°F (43° to 46°C). Add the yeast and stir until dissolved.
Let sit 5 to 10 minutes. The top will become slightly foamy.

Put the flour into a large bowl and make a well in the
center. Add the warm milk mixture and stir until well
blended and a soft dough forms. Cover the bowl with a dry
kitchen towel and let the dough rise in a warm place
(85°F/30°C) for 1 hour and 20 minutes, until doubled in volume.

In a small bowl, stir together the granulated sugar and
cinnamon. Set aside.

Dust a work surface lightly with flour and turn the dough
out onto it. Roll out dough into a rectangle 20 by 10 inches
(50 by 25 cm). Brush the top of the rectangle with 2 tablespoons
of the melted butter, then sprinkle evenly with the cinnamon
sugar, pecans, and raisins. Starting at a long side, roll up the
dough into a log. Cut the log into slices (like individual
cinnamon rolls) about 1 1/2 inches (4 cm) thick. You should have
about 14 slices.

Brush two 4 1/2-by-8 1/2-by-2 1/2-inch (11.5-by-21.5-by-6-cm)
loaf pans with 2 tablespoons of the melted butter. Arrange the
slices, standing them up vertically, in the prepared pans. Brush
the tops of the slices with the remaining 2 tablespoons melted
butter. Cover with a dry kitchen towel and let rise in a warm
place (85°F/30°C) for 45 to 60 minutes, until doubled in volume.
After 25 to 35 minutes, preheat the oven to 375°F (190°C).

Bake the loaves for about 30 minutes, until lightly browned
and a toothpick inserted into the center of a loaf comes out
clean. Let cool in the pans on wire racks for 5 minutes.

While the loaves are cooling, make the icing. In a glass
measuring pitcher, whisk together the powdered sugar and milk
until smooth. Gently turn the loaves out of the pans right side
up onto a serving platter and drizzle the sugar icing evenly onto
the warm loaves. Serve warm or at room temperature.

Banana Pecan Quick Bread

When new people move into the neighborhood, make it a tradition to deliver a loaf—the perfect size for gifting—of this moist, slightly sweet bread. When bananas take a turn from just right to past their prime, it's time to preheat the oven. Riper bananas make a more tender, more flavorful bread.

½ cup (125 ml) vegetable oil, plus more for
    greasing the pan

1¾ cups (280 g) all-purpose flour

2½ teaspoons baking powder

½ teaspoon salt

½ cup (105 g) firmly packed light brown sugar

1 large egg, lightly beaten

2 very ripe bananas, peeled and mashed

½ cup (125 ml) whole milk

½ teaspoon pure almond extract

½ cup (50 g) pecan halves, chopped

1 tablespoon poppy seeds

Preheat the oven to 350°F (180°C). Lightly grease a 4½-by-8½-by-2½-inch (11.5-by-21.5-by- 6-cm) loaf pan with oil.

In a bowl, whisk together the flour, baking powder, salt and brown sugar. In a second bowl, whisk together the egg, bananas, milk, oil, and almond extract until well blended. Add the egg mixture to the flour mixture and stir just until incorporated. Fold in the pecans and poppy seeds. Pour the batter into the prepared pan.

Bake for about 1 hour, until browned and a toothpick inserted into the center of the loaf comes out clean. Let cool in the pan on a wire rack for a few minutes, then turn out onto the rack and turn upright. Slice and serve warm or at room temperature.

Store any leftover bread tightly wrapped in aluminum foil at room temperature for up to 5 days.

Gathering Pecans, mural by Otis Dozier, 1941, Worthington National Bank, Arlington, Texas

Parmesan Pecan Popovers

By using cold ingredients, these herb-flavored pecan popovers rise dramatically and hold their shape after baking. They demand a lot of headroom as they bake, so be sure to place them in the middle of the oven without a rack above the pan. The dough is rich and hearty with eggs and pecans, making them a filling accompaniment to roast chicken or beef. Carry them to the table immediately after removing them from the oven, as they are best served steaming hot.

4 tablespoons (60 g) unsalted butter, melted
1¼ cups (310 ml) cold whole milk
4 cold large eggs, lightly beaten
½ cup (75 g) chilled all-purpose flour
½ cup (50 g) pecan halves, toasted and finely chopped
½ cup (60 g) freshly grated Parmigiano-Reggiano cheese
1½ teaspoons chopped fresh flat-leaf parsley
1½ teaspoons chopped fresh thyme
1 teaspoon chopped fresh rosemary
¼ teaspoon salt

Preheat the oven to 375°F (190°C). Brush the cups of a 6-cup popover pan with 3 tablespoons of the butter.

In a bowl, preferably with a spout, whisk together the milk, the remaining 1 tablespoon butter, and the eggs, blending well. Whisk in the flour, pecans, cheese, parsley, thyme, rosemary, and salt until well mixed.

Place the buttered popover pan in the preheated oven to heat for 3 minutes. Remove the hot pan from the oven and immediately pour or ladle the batter into the popover cups, dividing it evenly and filling each cup about three-fourths full. Bake for about 30 minutes, until popovers are extremely puffed and browned.

Turn the popovers out of the pan, slipping a knife around the edge of any popover that needs loosening, and serve immediately.

CORN AND PECAN SPOON BREAD

Spoon bread has been on southern tables for generations, though it's said to have been invented by Native Americans. With a corn bread–like taste and the airiness of a soufflé, it also conjures up savory French cuisine. Bake spoon bread right before serving and get it to the table quickly to show off its puff reminiscent of a soufflé. It's a dish that will work all day, from brunch served with eggs to dinner as an accompaniment to pork loin. If fresh corn is not in season, frozen will work fine.

Nonstick cooking spray, for the baking dish
2 cups (375 g) corn kernels (from about 3 ears)
2 cups (500 ml) whole milk
3/4 cup (115 g) yellow cornmeal
2 tablespoons unsalted butter, melted
2 teaspoons chopped fresh thyme
1 teaspoon salt
1/2 teaspoon freshly ground black pepper
4 large eggs, separated
1 cup (125 g) shredded sharp Cheddar cheese
3/4 cup (86 g) chopped pecans, toasted

Preheat the oven to 400°F (200°C). Lightly spray a 7-by-11-by-2-inch (18-by-28-by-5-cm) baking dish with cooking spray.

In a saucepan, combine the corn kernels, milk, and cornmeal and bring to a simmer over medium heat, stirring often. The mixture will be very thick. Transfer to a large bowl.

Stir in the butter, thyme, salt, and pepper, mixing well, then stir in the egg yolks until well blended. Add the cheese and pecans and stir until incorporated.

In another large bowl, using a handheld mixer, beat the egg whites on medium-high speed for 1 to 2 minutes, until stiff peaks form. Gently fold the beaten whites into the cornmeal mixture just until no white streaks remain. Pour the mixture into the prepared baking dish.

Bake for about 30 minutes, until puffed and browned. Serve immediately.

Starters & Snacks

Apricot and Honeyed Pecan Bites

One-bite appetizers allow people to mingle freely and nibble and are ideally passed at parties as guests are just arriving. Dainty yet satisfying, these are easy to eat and beautiful on a serving platter. The cheese should be sliced to fit neatly on top of the apricots. When herbs are starting to flower in the garden, add a blossom to each as a delicate garnish. Snip the blossoms and store them in an airtight container in the refrigerator for up to a week.

1 tablespoon roasted pecan oil

1 tablespoon honey

1/2 cup (50 g) pecan halves, toasted

24 whole dried apricots

24 slices Camembert cheese, each about 1 inch (2.5 cm) square and 1/8 inch (3 mm) thick

Flaky sea salt, such as Maldon, for sprinkling

Small fresh thyme sprigs or lavender flowers, for garnish

In a small bowl, stir together the oil and honey. Add the pecans and toss to coat evenly.

Arrange the apricots in a single layer on a platter. Top each apricot with a Camembert slice, trimming the cheese slightly, if needed to fit neatly, and top the cheese with a pecan half. Sprinkle with salt, garnish with thyme, and serve.

Pecan Sweet-Hot Mustard

This mustard evokes festive holiday buffets that center around glazed ham or roast beef with all the trimmings. Thanks to the added crunch of pecans and the sweet heat, you'll be hard-pressed to find any mustard that works in a sandwich as well as this inspired version. The mustard makes a wonderful gift, too, packed into small jars and decorated with a fancy plaid ribbon. For a smaller batch, halve the ingredients.

4 containers (2 ounces/60 g each) or 2 containers (4 ounces/125 g each) Colman's mustard powder

2 cups (500 ml) cider vinegar

2 cups (400 g) sugar

6 large egg yolks, lightly beaten

1/2 cup (50 g) pecan pieces, toasted and finely chopped

In a glass or other nonreactive bowl, whisk together the mustard powder and vinegar until well blended. Cover and let sit overnight at room temperature. The longer the mixture sits, the hotter the mustard will be.

In the top of a double boiler (or a heatproof bowl) set over (not touching) barely simmering water in the lower pan, combine the sugar and egg yolks and whisk together until completely mixed. Add the mustard-vinegar mixture and whisk constantly for 15 to 20 minutes, until the combined mixtures bubble and thicken. Remove from the heat and stir in the pecans, adding as much as you like.

Ladle the mustard into sterilized jars, cap tightly, and turn the jars upside down on a wire rack until cool. Store in the refrigerator for up to 1 month.

Funsten Holiday Pecans

MAKES 4 CUPS (400 G)

Named for the famed Funsten Nut Company in St. Louis, Missouri, these are a snap to make and call for only three ingredients. Serve them when someone stops by for a drink, wrap them in a cellophane bag with a pretty ribbon for a hostess gift, or offer them at a holiday party. No matter the occasion, your friends will be asking for the recipe every time!

1/2 cup (125 g) unsalted butter
4 cups (400 g) pecan halves
1/2 teaspoon salt

Preheat the oven to 350°F (180°C).

Put the butter on a large sheet pan and melt in the oven for 5 to 7 minutes. Add the pecans to the butter and stir until thoroughly coated. Return the pan to the oven and bake, stirring the pecans after about 6 minutes and again after about 12 minutes, for 18 to 20 minutes, until lightly browned.

Stir the pecans one more time, then transfer to paper towels to drain. Sprinkle with the salt while still warm, then let cool completely before serving.

Store the nuts in an airtight container at room temperature for up to 1 week, or in the refrigerator for up to 1 month.

Roasted Rosemary-Maple Pecans

MAKES 4 CUPS (400 G)

With a kiss of piney rosemary in each bite, these almost-candied pecans are hard to resist. Use the best maple syrup you can find. It fills each crevice of the nuts to create a memorable sweet glaze.

4 tablespoons unsalted butter
1/4 cup (90 g) pure maple syrup
1 tablespoon chopped fresh rosemary
1/2 teaspoon cayenne pepper
2 teaspoons salt
4 cups (400 g) pecan halves

Preheat the oven to 375°F (190°C). Line a large sheet pan with parchment paper.

In a saucepan, combine the butter, maple syrup, rosemary, and cayenne pepper and heat over low heat, just until the butter melts. Whisk to combine and remove from the heat. Add the pecans to the butter mixture and stir until thoroughly coated.

Transfer the pecans to the prepared sheet pan, spreading them in a single layer and scraping any remaining butter from the saucepan with a rubber spatula. Bake, stirring once after 6 or 7 minutes, for 13 to 15 minutes, until browned. Let cool completely on the pan on a wire rack before serving.

Store the nuts in an airtight container at room temperature for up to 1 week, or in the refrigerator for up to 1 month.

Endive Spears with Whipped Blue Cheese, Chives, and Pecans

There are nearly endless uses for Belgian endive. The leaves are slightly bitter, and they pair well with strong flavors like blue cheese. For this easy appetizer, the leaves are used as edible spoons. The smaller the endive head, the less bitter the flavor and easier the filled leaves are to arrange on a platter.

1 cup (100 g) pecan halves

2 tablespoons extra-virgin olive oil

1 teaspoon herbes de Provence

1/8 teaspoon salt

2 heads Belgian endive

8 ounces (250 g) crème fraîche

2 ounces (60 g) blue cheese, crumbled (about 1/2 cup)

2 tablespoons balsamic reduction (available at gourmet grocery stores)

3 tablespoons chopped fresh chives

Preheat the oven to 375°F (190°C). Place the pecans in a mound on the sheet pan, drizzle with the oil, and toss to coat evenly. Spread the pecans in a single layer and sprinkle with the herbs and salt. Bake for 10 minutes, until browned and fragrant. Pour onto a plate and let cool completely.

Slice off the base of each endive head to make the leaves easier to separate. Arrange the leaves, hollow side up, on a platter. You should have about 24 leaves.

In a bowl, using a handheld mixer, beat together the crème fraîche and blue cheese on medium speed for about 1 minute, until well mixed and stiff. Transfer the mixture to a resealable plastic bag, snip off a bottom corner of the bag, and pipe the mixture into the bottom 1 inch (2.5 cm) of each endive leaf.

Drizzle a little balsamic reduction over the crème fraîche mixture and on the upper part of each leaf. Sprinkle each mound of crème fraîche mixture with some of the chives and then top with a pecan half. Serve immediately.

CRISPY PECAN-CHEDDAR WAFERS

MAKES ABOUT **6** DOZEN WAFERS

These savory bite-size wafers are similar to classic southern cheese straws but are cut into pecan-studded coins. They pack an unbelievable amount of buttery richness from both the Cheddar cheese and the pecans. When cutting a chilled dough log, always rotate the log a quarter turn after each cut to help keep the slices perfectly round. Keep a well-wrapped log or two on hand in the freezer in case unexpected guests show up. The logs can be frozen for up to 1 month. Allow the dough to sit at room temperature for 30 minutes before slicing and baking.

2 cups (315 g) all-purpose flour
1 teaspoon salt
1/2 teaspoon cayenne pepper
1/2 cup (250 g) unsalted butter, at room temperature
2 cups (250 g) grated extra-sharp Cheddar cheese
1 cup (115 g) chopped pecans, toasted
1 large egg white, beaten until foamy

In the bowl of a stand mixer, whisk together the flour, salt, and cayenne pepper. Fit the mixer with the paddle attachment, add the butter and cheese, and beat on low speed until the ingredients are evenly mixed and the mixture comes together in a ball, about 3 minutes.

Divide the dough into four equal portions. Spread the pecans on a large plate. Place one portion of the dough on a sheet of waxed paper and, using your palms, shape it into a uniform log about 5 inches (13 cm) long. Brush the log on all sides with some of the egg white and then roll it in the pecans, coating it evenly. Gently press the pecans into the log with your fingertips, then wrap the log securely in the waxed paper.

Repeat with the remaining three dough portions. Chill the wrapped logs in the refrigerator for about 1 hour, until firm.

Preheat the oven to 325°F (165°F). Have ready an ungreased sheet pan.

Cut each log into slices 1/4 inch (6 mm) thick and arrange the slices on the sheet pan. Bake for 18 to 20 minutes, until lightly browned on top. Depending on the size of your pan, you may need to bake in two batches. Remove from the oven and carefully transfer the wafers to wire racks. Let cool completely.

Store the wafers in an airtight container at room temperature for up to 1 week.

Pecan *(Carya illinoinensis)*, watercolor by Bertha Heiges, 1904; Special Collections, USDA National Agricultural Library

A SWEET OR SAVORY SNACK

I have always loved pecans—they're an easy nut to love. Missouri pecans are different from the traditional larger pecans: they're tiny, extra sweet, and have a particularly bright flavor. I often use the Missouri northern variety because of their especially high oil content, which makes them sweeter and creamier. Eating them for the first time made me fall in love with pecans in a whole new way.

One of my favorite ways to use pecans is to candy them. I toss them in a very small amount of beaten egg white, sugar, salt, and cayenne pepper and roast them until browned. They're very simple but super delicious and addictive. At my restaurants, we'll top a dish with them or serve them in a little bowl as a snack. To showcase our local foods, I've made a Missouri wheat *agnolotti* with andouille sausage and topped the dish with these sweet and savory pecans. And to cross-pollinate, I'll also add *berbere*, an Ethiopian and Eritrean spice blend.

—Gerard Craft, Executive chef and owner of Niche Food Group, Niche Restaurant, Taste by Niche, Brasserie by Niche, Pastaria, Sardella, and Cinder House

CRÈME FRAÎCHE AND SMOKED GOUDA PECAN BALLS MAKES 2 BALLS

Nothing is wrong with your mother's cheese ball, but this one is better! Here's a modern version made with smoky Gouda and crème fraîche that is more intense and tangy than the traditional one. The raisins are unexpected but add the perfect touch of sweetness to the pecan-crusted smoked cheese.

1 package (8 ounces/250 g) cream cheese, at
    room temperature
1/2 pound (250 g) smoked Gouda cheese, shredded
1 container (8 ounces/250 g) crème fraîche
1/2 cup (75 g) golden raisins
2 teaspoons finely chopped fresh flat-leaf parsley
2 tablespoons minced shallot
1/8 teaspoon salt
1 1/4 cups (143 g) finely chopped pecans, toasted
Crackers, for serving

In a stand mixer fitted with the paddle attachment, combine the cream cheese, Gouda, crème fraîche, raisins, parsley, shallot, and salt and beat on medium-low speed until the ingredients are thoroughly combined and the mixture is creamy.

Divide the cheese mixture in half and shape each half into a ball. Spread the pecans on a plate and, one at a time, roll each ball in the pecans, coating it evenly. Wrap each ball loosely in waxed paper, slip the ball into a large resealable plastic bag, seal closed, and refrigerate for at least 2 hours or up to 3 days before serving. Serve the cheese balls with crackers.

Pecans and Sugarplums, painting © by Jean Townsend

WARM MUSTARD GREENS AND PECAN DIP

This refreshing new take on spinach dip is lightened by substituting Greek yogurt for some of the sour cream. If mustard greens aren't available, try kale or turnip greens. Whichever greens you choose, squeezing out as much moisture as possible from the leaves makes for the creamiest dip. Chill the mozzarella to make grating easier. This baked appetizer is best served with tortilla chips or baby vegetables for dipping.

1 package (12 ounces/375 g) fresh mustard greens

1 tablespoon extra-virgin olive oil

1 yellow onion, chopped

1 cup (250 g) sour cream

3/4 cup (185 g) plain whole-milk Greek yogurt

1 cup (100 g) pecan halves, toasted and chopped

1/2 pound (250 g) fresh mozzarella cheese, grated

1/2 teaspoon salt

1/8 teaspoon freshly ground black pepper

1/8 teaspoon cayenne pepper

Tortilla chips and/or baby vegetables, for serving

Preheat the oven to 350°F (180°C).

Bring a large saucepan of water to a boil, add the greens, and blanch for 3 minutes. Drain into a colander, rinse with cold running water until cool, and drain well. Wrap the greens with six layers of paper towels and squeeze repeatedly to remove as much moisture as possible. Unwrap and reserve.

In a frying pan, warm the oil over medium-low heat. Add the onion and cook, stirring occasionally, for about 5 minutes, until tender. Transfer to a large bowl. Add the blanched greens, sour cream, yogurt, pecans, mozzarella, salt, and black and cayenne peppers and mix until creamy and combined. Transfer to an 8-inch (20-cm) square baking dish with 2-inch (5-cm) sides.

Bake for about 30 minutes, until heated through and starting to brown around the edges. Serve warm with tortilla chips.

Sweet Potato Pecan Hummus

Hummus has become a popular alternative to cheese as an appetizer. In this fun variation, chickpeas have been swapped out for sweet potato and pecans and lime juice stands in for the usual lemon juice—and voilà, you have a healthy dip with a refreshing zing. It is also a great way to use up a leftover baked sweet potato. For the best result, pulse the pecans and garlic in the food processor until finely ground before adding the more substantial ingredients.

1 sweet potato, ¾ pound (375 g)
1 cup (100 g) pecan halves, toasted
1 clove garlic
¼ cup (45 g) tahini
3 tablespoons fresh lime juice
½ teaspoon salt
¼ teaspoon freshly ground black pepper
⅓ cup (80 ml) extra-virgin olive oil, plus more for finishing
Pinch of red pepper flakes
Sturdy crackers or baby vegetables, for serving

Preheat the oven to 400°F (200°C).

Wrap the sweet potato in aluminum foil. Place on a baking sheet and bake for about 1¼ hours, until soft in the center when pierced with a small, sharp knife. Let cool completely, peel, transfer to a bowl, and mash with a potato masher.

In a food processor, combine the pecans and garlic and pulse until finely ground. Add the mashed sweet potato, tahini, lime juice, salt, and black pepper and process until thoroughly combined and smooth. With the processor running, pour in the oil in a slow, steady stream.

Transfer the hummus to a serving bowl and finish with a drizzle of oil and the red pepper flakes. Serve with crackers.

Dolmades Stuffed with Minted Lamb and Pecans

Makes 3½ dozen dolmades

Dolmades are a Mediterranean appetizer and picnic staple found alongside olive bars in many upscale markets. This homemade version with lamb, pecans, and herbs will surpass any of the store-bought versions you've tried. Look for grape leaves alongside pickles in well-stocked grocery stores. When wrapping the leaves around the filling, make sure to leave a little space so the rice can expand during cooking without tearing the leaves.

1 jar (1 pound/500 g) grape leaves in vinegar brine
3 tablespoons pecan oil
1 yellow onion, finely chopped
1 clove garlic, minced
1 pound (500 g) ground lamb
⅓ cup (75 g) basmati rice
¼ cup (25 g) pecan halves, toasted and finely chopped
3 tablespoons chopped fresh flat-leaf parsley
1 tablespoon dried mint
1 teaspoon dried dill
Finely grated zest of 1 lemon
½ teaspoon salt
¼ teaspoon freshly ground black pepper
2 cups (500 ml) chicken broth
2 tablespoons fresh lemon juice
Lemon wedges, for serving

Drain the grape leaves, rinse well with cold water, and pat dry with paper towels.

In a frying pan, heat 2 tablespoons of the oil over medium-low heat. Add the onion and garlic and cook, stirring occasionally, for about 5 minutes, until tender. Remove from the heat and let cool.

In a bowl, combine the cooled onion mixture, lamb, rice, pecans, parsley, mint, dill, lemon zest, salt, and pepper and mix until all of the ingredients are evenly distributed.

Lay a grape leaf, shiny side down, on a flat surface. Place about 1 tablespoon of the lamb mixture near the stem end of the leaf. Fold the stem end over the lamb, then fold in both sides and roll up the leaf into a cigar shape, leaving room for the filling to expand as it cooks. Repeat with the remaining leaves and filling until you have used up all of the filling.

Arrange the dolmades, seam side down, on the bottom of a large Dutch oven. Snuggle the dolmades in very closely (you will not see the bottom of the pan) to make a single layer. Pour the broth, lemon juice, and the remaining 1 tablespoon oil evenly over the dolmades. Set on the stove top over low heat, cover, and simmer for about 1½ hours, until the rice is cooked and the leaves are tender. Serve warm or at room temperature with lemon wedges.

Store leftover dolmades in an airtight container in the refrigerator for up to 1 week; bring to room temperature before serving.

Dates Stuffed with Manchego and Pecans

The very talented chef Peter Dale makes dates similar to these as a starter for his fabulous meals at The National restaurant in Athens, Georgia. They are an entertaining staple, and a platter of these two-bite hors d'oeuvres fits well on nearly any party menu. Fresh dates are sold in the refrigerator section of some grocery stores and are worth the extra cost. Even though the dates are labeled pitted, double check to make sure no pits have been overlooked.

3/4 pound (375 g) pitted Medjool dates (about 18)
1 small fennel bulb
1 1/2 ounces (45 g) Manchego cheese
1/2 cup (50 g) pecan halves, toasted (about 18 halves)
Lemon olive oil, for drizzling
Smoked paprika, for garnish

Using a small, sharp knife, make a lengthwise slice in each date so it will open like a book.

Cut away the core and trim off the stems and fronds from the fennel bulb, reserving some of the fronds for garnish. Cut the fennel into thin pieces about the length of the dates. Cut the Manchego into pieces about 2 inches (5 cm) long by 1/2 inch (12 mm) wide by 1/8 inch (3 mm) thick. You will need about 18 pieces each of fennel and cheese.

Stuff each date with a piece each of fennel and cheese and a pecan half. Arrange on a platter. (If not serving right away, cover with plastic wrap and refrigerate, then bring to room temperature before serving.) Drizzle the dates with a little oil, sprinkle with paprika, and garnish with the reserved fennel fronds, then serve.

Arugula and Pecan Pizzette

Pizzette *are small, single-serving pizzas that make a nice first course or light lunch. Fresh refrigerated pizza dough is available in many grocery stores and requires just a little rolling before topping and baking, or you might ask your local pizzeria to sell you a small amount of dough. Piling frilly arugula on top of the warm pizzette just before serving adds color and a peppery bite that perfectly complements the rustic pecan topping.*

1 pound (500 g) fresh pizza dough
All-purpose flour, for the work surface
2 tablespoons olive oil
9 ounces (270 g) Fontina cheese, shredded
1/4 pound (125 g) sliced prosciutto, torn into bite-size pieces
2 cups (200 g) pecan halves, toasted and roughly chopped
1/4 pound (125 g) baby arugula
Aged balsamic vinegar, for drizzling

Place two sheet pans in the oven and preheat the oven to 400°F (200°C).

Cut the pizza dough into four equal portions. Dust a work surface with flour and roll out each dough portion into a round about 5 inches (13 cm) in diameter. Prick each dough round several times with a fork.

Using a wide spatula, carefully transfer the dough rounds to the hot pans. Bake for 5 to 6 minutes, until just starting to brown. Remove from the oven and top each round evenly, in the following order, with one-fourth each of the oil, cheese, prosciutto, and pecans. Return to the oven and bake for about 15 minutes, until cheese is melted and edges of crust are browned.

Remove the pizzette from the oven and transfer them to individual plates or a large platter. Top each with one-fourth of the arugula, drizzle lightly with vinegar, and serve.

SALADS & SIDE DISHES

Pecan Oil Vinaigrettes

Vinaigrettes taste best the day they are made. If some vinaigrette is left over, cover and refrigerate and try to use it within a day or two. The pecan oil will solidify when chilled, so bring the dressing to room temperature and whisk well before serving.

Pomegranate Molasses Pecan Vinaigrette

2/3 cup (80 ml) pecan oil
3 tablespoons red wine vinegar
3 tablespoons pomegranate molasses
1 teaspoon Dijon mustard
Salt and freshly ground black pepper

In a small bowl, whisk together the oil, vinegar, pomegranate molasses, and mustard until well blended. Season with salt and pepper.

Thyme and Shallot Pecan Vinaigrette

2/3 cup (80 ml) pecan oil
3 tablespoons white wine vinegar
1 tablespoon Dijon mustard
1/2 shallot, finely diced
1 1/2 teaspoons fresh thyme leaves, chopped
Salt and freshly ground black pepper

In a small bowl, whisk together the oil, vinegar, mustard, shallot, and thyme until well blended. Season with salt and pepper.

Kalamata Pecan Vinaigrette

2/3 cup (80 ml) pecan oil
3 tablespoons red wine vinegar
1/2 teaspoon Dijon mustard
1/2 cup (75 g) pitted Kalamata olives, chopped
1 1/2 teaspoons fresh rosemary leaves, chopped
1 clove garlic, minced

In a small bowl, whisk together all of the ingredients until well blended.

Grilled Romaine with Blue Cheese and Pecan Dressing

After the main course is off the grill, use the last few minutes of heat for this salad. Grilling the lettuce for just a few minutes is a great way to add an unexpected seasoning. The fire imparts smoky flavor to each romaine heart while the hint of char on the leaves adds texture. Toasted pecans give the creamy dressing the perfect added crunch.

3 hearts romaine lettuce, about 3/4 pound (375 g) total
2 bunches green onions (12 onions)
2 tablespoons pecan oil

Dressing
2/3 cup (160 ml) pecan oil
1/3 cup (80 ml) fresh lemon juice
1 teaspoon Dijon mustard
1/2 teaspoon salt
1/4 teaspoon freshly ground black pepper
1/4 cup (40 g) crumbled good-quality blue cheese
1/2 cup (60 g) pecans, toasted and chopped

Chopped fresh chives, for garnish

Pull off the tough outer leaves from the romaine hearts and discard. Cut each heart in half lengthwise, keeping the leaves intact. Trim off the root ends and about 1/2 inch (12 mm) of the green ends from the green onions. Brush the lettuce and onions evenly with the oil.

To make the dressing, whisk together the oil, lemon juice, mustard, salt, and pepper. Stir in the cheese and pecans and set aside.

Prepare a medium-low fire (300°F/150°C) in a charcoal or gas grill. Place the green onions on the cooking grate, close the grill lid, and grill for 2 to 3 minutes, until slightly charred. Transfer the onions to a plate.

Place the romaine halves, cut side down, on the cooking grate. Grill, with lid open, for 2 to 3 minutes, until wilted and just beginning to show grill marks. Remove from the heat.

Divide the grilled lettuce halves among six serving plates. Top with the green onions and drizzle with the dressing. Garnish with chives and serve immediately.

Texas Cobb Salad with Chipotle Pecans

Cobb Salad has been an American signature salad since its creation in the late 1930s. First served at the Brown Derby restaurant in Hollywood, California, the salad was named for the owner, Robert Cobb. This Tex-Mex version is a combination of gorgeous colors and spices. The chipotle-spiced pecans can also be served on their own as a snack or as a nibble at your next party.

Chipotle Pecans

3 tablespoons unsalted butter

2 teaspoons adobo sauce from canned chipotle chiles in adobo sauce

1 teaspoon chipotle chile powder

1/2 teaspoon salt

2 cups (200 g) pecan halves

Dressing

3/4 cup (180 ml) mayonnaise

1/2 cup (125 ml) buttermilk

3 tablespoons chopped fresh cilantro

Finely grated zest of 2 limes

1/4 teaspoon salt

1/4 teaspoon freshly ground black pepper

1 head green leaf lettuce, chopped or torn into bite-size pieces

1/2 large red onion, finely chopped

1 pint (280 g) cherry tomatoes, stemmed and halved

2 avocados, halved, pitted, peeled, and cut into cubes

6 ounces (185 g) pepper Jack cheese, shredded

3/4 pound (375 g) bacon, cooked until crisp, drained, and crumbled

To make the chipotle pecans, preheat the oven to 350°F (180°C). Line a large sheet pan with parchment paper.

In a saucepan, combine the butter, adobo sauce, chile powder, and salt and heat over low heat until melted, whisking to combine. Add the pecans and stir until evenly coated. Transfer the pecans to the prepared pan, spreading them in a single layer and using a rubber spatula to scrape all of the butter from the saucepan.

Roast the pecans, stirring once after 7 or 8 minutes, for about 15 minutes, until browned and fragrant. Pour onto a plate and let cool. (The pecans will keep in an airtight container at room temperature for up to 1 week, or in the refrigerator for up to 1 month.)

To make the dressing, in a small bowl, whisk together all of the ingredients. Cover and refrigerate until ready to use. (The dressing can be made up to 2 days in advance.)

Make a bed of the lettuce on a large serving platter. Arrange the onion, tomatoes, avocados, cheese, and bacon in decorative stripes on top of the lettuce. Drizzle with the dressing, top with the pecans, and serve immediately.

Mixed Spring Greens with Blueberries, Goat Cheese, and Cinnamon-Spiced Pecans

A warm-weather salad with a classic vinaigrette is a recipe that all cooks should have in their collection. Almost any protein can be added to this adaptable version to create a complete meal full of color. For a prettier presentation, arrange the toppings on the greens in a large bowl or platter, drizzle the dressing over the salad, and toss just before serving. Make a double batch of the spiced pecans, as they tend to disappear quickly.

Cinnamon-Spiced Pecans

4 tablespoons (55 g) coconut oil

1/4 cup (50 g) sugar

2 teaspoons ground cinnamon

1/2 teaspoon cayenne pepper

1/2 teaspoon salt

2 cups (200 g) pecan halves

1/2 pound (250 g) mixed salad greens

1 cup (155 g) blueberries

2 ounces (60 g) fresh goat cheese, crumbled

3 tablespoons balsamic vinegar

1 teaspoon Dijon mustard

1/4 teaspoon salt

1/4 teaspoon freshly ground black pepper

1/2 cup (125 ml) extra-virgin olive oil

To make the spiced pecans, preheat the oven to 350°F (180°C). Line a large sheet pan with parchment paper.

In a saucepan, combine the coconut oil, sugar, cinnamon, cayenne pepper, and salt and heat over low heat until melted, whisking to combine. Add the pecans and stir until thoroughly coated. Transfer the pecans to the prepared pan, spreading them in a single layer and using a rubber spatula to scrape all of the butter from the saucepan.

Roast the pecans, stirring once after 7 or 8 minutes, until browned. Pour onto a plate and let cool. (The pecans will keep in an airtight container at room temperature for up to 1 week, or in the refrigerator for up to 1 month.)

Make a bed of the lettuce in a large bowl or serving platter. Scatter the berries and goat cheese evenly over the top. In a glass measuring pitcher, whisk together the vinegar, mustard, salt, and pepper. Slowly add the oil while whisking vigorously. Drizzle the dressing over the salad, top with the spiced pecans, and serve immediately.

ASIAN SLAW WITH MISO-PECAN DRESSING

This slaw is bursting with umami, and because it contains no mayonnaise, it's ideal for tailgates and picnics. When chopping the cilantro, include some of the stems, as they actually have more flavor than their leafy tops. You'll have a little extra dressing left over, so try it with crudités or drizzle it over shrimp or fried chicken.

DRESSING

¼ cup (60 g) Dijon mustard

½ cup (125 ml) white wine vinegar

3 tablespoons white miso

2 tablespoons sugar

1 tablespoon soy sauce

¼ teaspoon salt

¼ teaspoon freshly ground black pepper

2 tablespoons extra-virgin olive oil

2 tablespoons toasted sesame oil

⅓ cup (33 g) pecan halves, toasted and chopped

6 cups (560 g) thinly sliced napa cabbage

1 red bell pepper, seeded and cut lengthwise into narrow strips

1 serrano chile, seeded and cut lengthwise into narrow strips

1 carrot, peeled and cut lengthwise into ribbons with a vegetable peeler

3 green onions, white and light green parts, sliced

2 tablespoons chopped fresh cilantro

To make the dressing, in a small bowl, whisk together the mustard, vinegar, miso, sugar, soy sauce, salt, and pepper. Slowly add the olive and sesame oils while whisking vigorously. Stir in the pecans.

In a large serving bowl, combine the cabbage, bell pepper, chile, carrot, green onions, and cilantro. Drizzle with the dressing to taste; you may not need all of it. Toss the salad, coating the ingredients evenly, and serve immediately.

SOBA NOODLE SALAD WITH RADISHES AND PECAN SAUCE

Japanese soba noodles are made from buckwheat flour, which gives them a beautiful brown color. To make the pecan sauce just the way you like it, blend the nuts in a food processor until the texture is silky smooth or slightly chunky. This sauce is also good as a dip for egg rolls and alongside grilled chicken.

PECAN SAUCE

2-inch (5-cm) piece fresh ginger, peeled and chopped

2 cloves garlic

1/4 cup (78 g) pecan butter (page 33)

1/4 cup (60 ml) soy sauce

3 tablespoons pecan oil

2 tablespoons dry sherry

2 tablespoons honey

1 tablespoon pure toasted sesame oil

1 tablespoon white wine vinegar

1/2 teaspoon Sriracha sauce

Juice of 1 lime

1/2 cup (58 g) chopped pecans, toasted

1 package (12 ounces/375 g) dried soba noodles, cooked according to package directions, drained

3 radishes, thinly sliced

1/2 jalapeño chile, seeded and thinly sliced crosswise

1 red bell pepper, seeded and julienned

1 yellow bell pepper, seeded and julienned

4 green onions, white and light green parts, thinly sliced, plus more for garnish

Fresh cilantro sprigs, for garnish

Lime wedges, for garnish

To make the sauce, in a food processor or blender, combine the ginger and garlic and pulse until minced. Add the pecan butter, soy sauce, pecan oil, sherry, honey, sesame oil, vinegar, Sriracha, and lime juice and process until smooth. Add the pecans and pulse until you achieve the texture you like. (The sauce will keep in an airtight container in the refrigerator for up to 1 week.)

In a large serving bowl, combine the noodles, radishes, chile, bell peppers, and green onions and toss to mix. Add the sauce and toss to coat the noodles and vegetables evenly. Garnish with cilantro, lime wedges, and green onions and serve.

OLD-FASHIONED SOUTHERN CHICKEN SALAD WITH TOASTED PECANS

Southern bridal showers and ladies' lunches aren't complete without homemade chicken salad. Women in the South typically rely on a recipe that has been famous in their family for generations. Pecans are so common in chicken salads east of the Mississippi that when a nut-free version is served, it just doesn't feel right.

4 cups (560 g) chopped cooked chicken
1/2 cup (125 ml) mayonnaise
1/2 teaspoon Dijon mustard
1/2 sweet onion, diced
Juice of 1 lemon
1/2 cup (58 g) chopped pecans, toasted
1 tablespoon chopped fresh flat-leaf parsley
1/4 teaspoon salt
1/8 teaspoon freshly ground black pepper

Combine all of the ingredients in a large bowl and mix well. Cover and chill for 2 hours before serving.

Pecans in Arnaudville, painting © by Lue Svendson

Red Beans and Brown Basmati Rice Drizzled with Pecan Oil

SERVES 8

Eating red beans and rice on Mondays is a long-standing New Orleans tradition. Generations ago, cooking the Creole favorite the day after the Sabbath was an economical way to finish off the Sunday ham. This comforting ritual still stands today. If you don't have time to soak the beans overnight, cover them with water, bring to a boil, remove from the heat, and let sit for 1 hour, then drain and proceed as directed. Serve the beans over rice and drizzle each portion with a little extra pecan oil.

6 tablespoons (90 ml) pecan oil, plus more for finishing
2 cloves garlic, minced
2 celery stalks, diced
1 yellow onion, diced
1 green bell pepper, seeded and diced
5 cups (1.1 l) water
1 bag (1 pound/500 g) dried red beans (generous 2 cups), picked over, soaked overnight in water to cover, and drained
2 fresh bay leaves
2 teaspoons fresh thyme leaves, chopped
1 teaspoon fresh oregano leaves, chopped
1 teaspoon hot smoked paprika

2 cups (500 ml) chicken broth
1 teaspoon salt
1/4 teaspoon freshly ground black pepper
1/2 cup (58 g) chopped pecans, toasted
Freshly cooked brown basmati rice, for serving
Green onions, white and light green parts, sliced, for garnish
Fresh red chiles, sliced, for garnish
Hot sauce, for serving

In a Dutch oven, heat 2 tablespoons of the oil over medium heat. Add the garlic, celery, onion, and bell pepper and cook, stirring occasionally, for about 10 minutes, until the vegetables are tender. Add the water, red beans, bay leaves, thyme, oregano, paprika, and the remaining 4 tablespoons (60 ml) oil and stir well. Cook uncovered, stirring occasionally, for 30 minutes. Add the broth, salt, and pepper, raise the heat to medium-high, and bring to a boil. Reduce the heat to a simmer and cook uncovered, stirring occasionally, for about 1 hour, until the beans are tender.

Turn off the heat and remove and discard the bay leaves. Add the pecans and stir to combine. Spoon the rice into large individual bowls and ladle the beans over the top. Drizzle each serving with a little oil, garnish with green onions and chiles, and serve immediately. Pass hot sauce at the table.

Roasted Poblano Chiles Stuffed with Quinoa, Corn, and Pecans

Quinoa, an ancient grain now being rightfully touted as a superfood, forms the base for the filling of these glorious Southwest-inspired stuffed chiles. Using poblanos instead of bell peppers adds more heat and flavor, and they're large enough to stand alone as a vegetarian main course. They also travel well, making them a good choice if you're assigned to bring a hefty side dish to a potluck dinner. Be prepared to bring copies of this recipe, too, as you're sure to be getting requests!

To save time the day of serving, assemble the stuffed chiles a day ahead and then bake them straight from the fridge, adding about 10 minutes to the cooking time. If you cannot find Mexican crema, a slightly soured, lightly thickened cream, crème fraîche can be substituted.

12 large poblano chiles
1 cup (185) tricolor quinoa
2 cups (500 ml) vegetable broth
Nonstick cooking spray, for the baking dish
2 tablespoons pecan oil
2 cups (375 g) corn kernels (from about 3 ears)
1 small white onion, chopped
1 teaspoon chili powder
1/2 teaspoon ground cumin
1/4 teaspoon red pepper flakes
1/4 teaspoon salt
1/2 cup (58 g) chopped pecans, toasted
2 cups (250 g) shredded Monterey Jack cheese
1/4 cup (10 g) chopped fresh cilantro, plus sprigs for garnish
Mexican crema, for serving

Position an oven rack 4 to 6 inches (10 to 15 cm) from the heat source and preheat the broiler. Place the poblanos on a broiler pan or sheet pan, slip the pan under the broiler, and broil, turning the chiles as needed to color evenly, for 8 to 12 minutes, until the skins blacken and blister. Remove from the broiler, transfer to a heatproof plastic bag, seal closed, and let stand for 15 minutes.

Remove the chiles from the bag and gently peel away the blackened skins. Beginning about 1 inch (2.5 cm) from the stem, cut a lengthwise slit to the bottom of each chile. Gently remove and discard the seeds, leaving the stem intact and being careful not to tear the walls of the chiles. Set aside.

Put the quinoa in a fine-mesh sieve and rinse under cold running water. Transfer to a saucepan and cook according to the package directions, using the broth instead of water. Set aside.

Preheat the oven to 350°F (180°C). Spray a 13-by-9-inch (33-by-23-cm) baking dish with cooking spray.

In a frying pan, heat the oil over medium heat. Add the corn, onion, chili powder, cumin, red pepper flakes, and salt and cook, stirring often, for about 5 minutes, until the onion is tender. Stir in the quinoa and cook, stirring often, for 2 minutes. Stir in the pecans, 1 cup (125 g) of the cheese, and the cilantro and remove from the heat.

(continued next page)

The word *pecan* comes from an Algonquian word meaning "nut requiring a stone to crack." Wild crows that foraged for the nuts could break open the hard outer shell. The crows (as well as squirrels and other animals) then helped the pecan migrate westward by dispersing the nuts in flight. As long as the endosperm wasn't damaged, the fruit could propagate, and that is how the pecan spread into Oklahoma, Texas, and New Mexico. Today, it is the number-one nut crop in New Mexico.

The pecan is a species of hickory native to the United States and Mexico, and the trees can live and bear edible fruits for over three hundred years. Like the fruit of other members of the hickory genus, the pecan is not a true nut, but a rich, buttery fruit with a single stone or pit surrounded by a husk.

With 690 calories per 100 grams, pecans were an important source of protein to many early Native American tribes, who both consumed and traded them. When wild game was scarce, the nuts, which could be eaten both raw and cooked, provided an important source of calories and unsaturated fat.

—LOIS ELLEN FRANK, Ph.D.,
chef-owner of Red Mesa Cuisine,
Native American cooking instructor, and author
of *Foods of the Southwest Indian Nations*

ROASTED POBLANO CHILES STUFFED WITH QUINOA, CORN, AND PECANS (CONTINUED)

Divide the quinoa mixture evenly among the poblanos, stuffing them gently to avoid tears. Arrange the poblanos, cut side up, in the prepared baking dish. Sprinkle the filling with the remaining 1 cup (125 g) cheese, dividing it evenly.

Bake for 15 to 20 minutes, until the filling is heated through and the cheese has melted. Serve immediately, garnished with crema and cilantro.

Pacanenut Hickory, 1841, by Henri-Joseph Redouté

New Mexico Sweet Potatoes with Chiles, Cilantro, and Pecans

We are indebted to the Native Americans for pecans, and this New Mexican recipe pays homage to them and our Mexican neighbors. How lucky we are to have inherited such a rich culinary heritage from these two cultures. You may think of chiles when you think of New Mexican agriculture, but pecans are the state's number-one food crop and figure prominently in the local cuisine.

These potatoes are divine! Be sure to bake them on two sheet pans to ensure they turn out well roasted and sturdy enough to be tossed and coated with the sauce. Crowding them onto one pan will yield steamed potatoes instead of browned wedges. Serve them alongside burgers, grilled salmon, or roast pork loin and garnish them with lots of lime.

4 uniform-size sweet potatoes, each about 3/4 pound (375 g)

3 tablespoons extra-virgin olive oil

3/4 teaspoon salt

1/4 teaspoon freshly ground black pepper

4 tablespoons (60 g) unsalted butter

1/4 cup (90 g) honey

1 chipotle chile in adobo sauce, diced, plus 1 teaspoon adobo sauce

1/4 teaspoon ground cinnamon

1/4 cup (28 g) chopped pecans

1/4 cup (5 g) fresh cilantro leaves

2 limes, quartered, for garnish

Preheat the oven to 425°F (220°C).

Scrub the unpeeled sweet potatoes well with cold water, then cut lengthwise into wedges about 1 inch (2.5 cm) wide. Divide the wedges evenly between two sheet pans, drizzle each half with half of the oil, toss to coat evenly, then sprinkle with 1/2 teaspoon of the salt and the pepper. Spread the wedges on the pans, leaving space around each piece. Bake for about 30 minutes, until almost tender when pierced with a fork.

Meanwhile, in a small saucepan, combine the butter, honey, chipotle chile, adobo sauce, cinnamon, and the remaining 1/4 teaspoon salt and set over low heat. When the butter has melted, stir well, add the pecans, and cook, stirring occasionally, for about 10 minutes, until the flavors are well blended. Set aside.

Remove the potatoes from the oven and consolidate them onto one sheet pan. Spoon the butter mixture over the potatoes and toss to coat. Return the pan to the oven and bake for about 8 minutes longer, until the potatoes are tender when pierced with a fork.

Let the potatoes cool for 3 minutes, then arrange them on a large platter. Garnish with the cilantro and lime wedges and serve warm.

Pancetta Brussels Sprouts with Pecan Dusting Serves 6

This roasted side dish is simple to make, beautiful on the plate, and an essential for any Thanksgiving menu. Roasting the Brussels sprouts at such a high temperature caramelizes and crisps them to an irresistible texture. When shopping for Brussels sprouts, look for plump ones with tightly packed leaves. They are loaded with nutrition and require little preparation to become a memorable side dish.

1½ pounds (750 g) Brussels sprouts
4 tablespoons (60 ml) extra-virgin olive oil
¼ pound (125 g) pancetta or thick-cut bacon, chopped
2 shallots, thinly sliced
2 tablespoons very finely chopped pecans ¾ teaspoon salt
½ teaspoon freshly ground black pepper

Preheat the oven to 450°F (230°C). Remove discolored or loose outer leaves from each Brussels sprout and trim the stem flush with the base. Cut the sprouts in half lengthwise and set aside.

In a large frying pan, heat 1 tablespoon of the oil over medium heat. Add the pancetta and shallots and cook, stirring often, for about 6 minutes, until browned and crispy. Using a slotted spoon, transfer the pancetta and shallots to a plate.

Add the pecans to the oil remaining in the pan, reduce the heat to low, and cook, stirring often, for 2 to 3 minutes, until lightly browned. Transfer to a small dish and set aside.

Pile the Brussels sprouts on a large sheet pan, drizzle with the remaining 3 tablespoons oil, and toss to coat evenly with the oil. Arrange the sprouts, cut side down, in a single layer on the pan. Sprinkle with the salt and pepper.

Roast for 12 to 15 minutes, until deeply browned. Remove from the oven, add the pancetta and shallots, and stir together, mixing well. Transfer to a serving dish, top with the pecans, and serve immediately.

Sautéed Green Beans with Black Olives and Pecans

Salty olives and crunchy pecans add extra color, texture, and taste to this versatile side dish that goes with just about any main course. It also requires just one pan, saving time and cleanup.

1 pound (500 g) green beans, trimmed

⅓ cup (80 ml) water

1 tablespoon pecan oil

½ cup (58 g) chopped pecans, toasted

½ cup (75 g) Kalamata or oil-cured black olives, pitted and halved

1 tablespoon chopped fresh flat-leaf parsley

½ teaspoon salt

¼ teaspoon freshly ground black pepper

In a large frying pan or sauté pan with a lid, combine the beans and water and bring to a boil over high heat. Cover and cook for 5 minutes.

Uncover and cook for about 2 minutes longer, until all of the water has evaporated. Carefully add the oil (it may spatter) and sauté the beans for 2 minutes. Stir in the pecans, olives, parsley, salt, and pepper and sauté for 1 minute longer, until the beans are just tender.

Transfer to a serving bowl or platter and serve immediately.

HEIRLOOM TOMATO PIE WITH PECAN-PARMESAN CRUST   SERVES 8

When summer tomatoes are at their peak of flavor, use them to fill a rustic pecan meal crust to create a beautiful savory pie. This takes some time to prepare, but is definitely worth it! The crust hugs the tomatoes as it bakes, so don't worry about having a perfect circle when rolling out your dough.

CRUST

2 cups (315 g) all-purpose flour, plus more for the
    work surface and kneading
¼ cup (28 g) pecan meal (page 32)
1 tablespoon baking powder
1 teaspoon kosher salt
1 cup (250 g) cold unsalted butter, cut into cubes
½ cup (125 g) crème fraîche
¼ cup (30 g) freshly grated Parmigiano-Reggiano cheese

FILLING

3 pounds (1.5 kg) heirloom tomatoes in assorted colors
1 teaspoon kosher salt
1½ cups (185 g) shredded extra-sharp Cheddar cheese
½ cup (60 g) freshly grated Parmigiano-Reggiano cheese
½ cup (125 ml) mayonnaise
1 large egg, lightly beaten
2 tablespoons chopped fresh flat-leaf parsley
1 tablespoon fresh thyme leaves, chopped
1 tablespoon cider vinegar
1 shallot, chopped
2 teaspoons sugar
¼ teaspoon freshly ground black pepper
1½ tablespoons yellow cornmeal

TOPPING

⅓ (38 g) cup finely chopped pecans
2 tablespoons freshly grated Parmigiano-Reggiano cheese
1 teaspoon fresh thyme, chopped

To make the crust, in the bowl of a stand mixer, whisk together the flour, pecan meal, baking powder, and salt until blended. Scatter the butter over the flour mixture and, using a pastry blender or two knives, cut in the butter until the mixture forms coarse crumbs the size of small peas. Add the crème fraîche and cheese, fit the mixer with the paddle attachment, and beat on low speed for about 1 minute, until the mixture comes together in a rough dough-like mass.

Dust a work surface generously with flour and transfer the dough to it. Sprinkle the dough lightly with flour and knead, folding it over on itself and pressing down with the heels of your hands, three or four times, until it comes together, adding more flour as needed. Do not overwork the dough or the crust will be tough. Roll out the dough into a 14-inch (35-cm) round.

Cover the outside of a 9 ½-inch (24-cm) springform pan with heavy-duty foil. This helps to prevent any possible leaking from the pan. Carefully roll the dough around the rolling pin, brushing off any excess flour, and position the pin over the prepared pan. Unroll the dough, centering it in the pan, and gently press it onto the bottom and up the sides.

(continued next page)

The crust edges will be uneven (and will be pretty that way). If any dough hangs over the pan rim, tear it off even with the rim. Chill the crust for 30 minutes.

To make the filling, cut two-thirds of the tomatoes into slices ¼ inch (6 mm) thick and remove the seeds from the slices. Arrange the slices in a single layer on paper towels and sprinkle evenly with salt. Let stand for 30 minutes.

Preheat the oven to 425°F (220°C). In a bowl, combine the Cheddar and Parmigiano-Reggiano cheeses, mayonnaise, egg, parsley, thyme, vinegar, shallot, sugar, and pepper and stir until well blended.

Pat the tomato slices dry with paper towels. Sprinkle the cornmeal evenly over the bottom of the crust. Lightly spread 1 cup (200 g) of the cheese mixture onto the crust. Pat the tomato slices dry with paper towels and layer half of the slices, in slightly overlapping rows, on top of the cheese mixture. Spread the tomato layer with ½ cup (100 g) of the cheese mixture. Repeat the layers, using the remaining tomato slices and cheese mixture. Cut the remaining tomatoes into slices ¼ inch (6 mm) thick and arrange on top of the final cheese-mixture layer.

To make the topping, in a small bowl, combine all of the ingredients, mixing well. Set aside.

Bake the pie for 50 minutes. Sprinkle the topping evenly over the pie and continue to bake for about 20 minutes, until golden brown. Let cool completely in the pan on a wire rack.

To serve, unclasp and remove the side rim of the pan and cut into wedges.

We Buy Pecans, Cairo, Georgia, 2018; painting © by Tracy Foutz-Hunt

Wild Rice with Mushrooms and Pecans

In a book celebrating pecans, our American nut, it seems only right to include a recipe that combines the nuts with wild rice, one of only two grains native to North America. Serve this easy side dish with roast chicken for a weeknight supper or alongside a beef tenderloin when entertaining a crowd. Assemble the dish early in the day or a day ahead, refrigerate, and bake just before serving. The leftovers are great hot with a fried egg on top, or cold as a base for rice salad.

5 tablespoons (75 g) unsalted butter, plus more for greasing the pan

1 cup (185 g) wild rice

1 pound (500 g) small white mushrooms, stemmed and quartered lengthwise

1 yellow onion, chopped

1 clove garlic, minced

1 cup (115 g) chopped pecans, toasted

3 cups (750 ml) chicken broth

2 tablespoons dry sherry

1 teaspoon salt

1/2 teaspoon freshly ground black pepper

Preheat the oven to 350°F (180°C). Grease a shallow 2-quart (2 l) lidded baking dish with butter.

Put the wild rice into a fine-mesh sieve and rinse well under cold running water. Drain and set aside.

In a large frying, melt 2 tablespoons of the butter over medium-low heat. Add the mushrooms and sauté for 3 to 4 minutes, until they are browned and release their juices. Continue to cook for about 10 minutes longer, until the juices are reduced and the pan is nearly dry. Transfer the mushrooms to a platter and return the unwashed pan to the stove top over medium-low heat.

Add 2 tablespoons of the butter to the pan. When the butter melts, add the onion and garlic and cook, stirring occasionally, for 2 to 3 minutes, until the onion is translucent. Transfer the onion and garlic to the platter with the mushrooms.

Return the unwashed pan to the stove top over medium heat. Add the remaining 1 tablespoon butter and the pecans and cook, stirring often, for about 2 minutes, until fragrant and toasted. Stir in the wild rice, broth, sherry, mushrooms, onion, garlic, salt, and pepper, mixing well.

Transfer the rice mixture to the prepared baking dish and top with lid. Bake for about 1½ hours, until the rice is just tender. Drain off any excess liquid and serve hot.

Main Courses

Zucchini, Broccoli, Bell Pepper, and Pecan Stir-Fry

Nearly any vegetable can be used in this impressively fragrant stir-fry. The hoisin and chile sauces combine to make a balanced and refined dish. Use pecan halves instead of pieces, as they won't get lost in the rainbow of colors on the plate. Serve immediately with white or brown rice as a vegetarian main course. Any stir-fry moves quickly once you turn on the heat, so have all of the vegetables sliced and ingredients measured, including the broth mixture, before you begin to cook.

3 tablespoons vegetable oil

2 medium zucchini, trimmed and sliced

1 large red bell pepper, seeded and cut lengthwise into ¼-inch strips

4 cloves garlic, sliced

1 pound (500 g) broccoli florets

4 tablespoons (60 ml) soy sauce

1½ tablespoons Asian chile sauce

1 tablespoon hoisin sauce

2 cups (500 ml) chicken broth

2 tablespoons cornstarch

1 cup (100 g) pecan halves, toasted

3 cups (470 g) freshly cooked rice, for serving

Heat a wok or large frying pan over high heat for 2 to 3 minutes, until very hot. Add the oil and swirl the pan to coat the bottom and sides with oil. Add the zucchini, bell pepper, garlic, and broccoli and cook, stirring frequently, for 2 minutes. Add 2 tablespoons of the soy sauce and cook for 1 minute, stirring constantly. Add the chile and hoisin sauces and cook, stirring, for about 3 minutes, until the broccoli is tender.

In a bowl, whisk together the broth, cornstarch, and the remaining 2 tablespoons soy sauce. Slowly add the broth mixture to the pan while stirring constantly. Continue to cook, stirring, for about 3 minutes, until the sauce thickens. Stir in the pecans and remove from the heat.

Divide the rice among individual plates or bowls and spoon the stir-fry over the top. Serve immediately.

Pasta with Butternut Squash, Pancetta, Pecans, and Fried Sage Leaves

Sage and pecans have long been a classic pairing. The herb-infused olive oil created from frying the sage is absorbed by the pasta, delivering an extra-aromatic flavor that marries perfectly with toasted pecans and slightly sweet winter squash. Cooking the squash for a little less time than you typically would ensures its texture holds up when you toss it with the hot pasta just before serving.

1 large butternut squash, about 3 pounds (1.5 kg), halved, seeded, peeled, and cut into 1/2-inch (12-mm) pieces

3 tablespoons plus 1/4 cup (60 ml) extra-virgin olive oil

3/4 teaspoon salt

1/2 teaspoon freshly ground black pepper

1/4 pound (125 g) pancetta, chopped

1/2 cup (20 g) panko bread crumbs

Leaves from 1 bunch sage (about 24 leaves)

2 tablespoons unsalted butter

1 pound (500 g) dried fusilli pasta

1 cup (100 g) pecan halves, toasted

2 tablespoons chopped fresh flat-leaf parsley

3/4 cup (90 g) freshly grated Parmigiano-Reggiano cheese

Preheat the oven to 400°F (200°C). Mound the squash on a large sheet pan, drizzle with 1 tablespoon of the oil, and toss to coat evenly. Spread the squash pieces in a single layer and sprinkle with the salt and pepper. Roast, turning the pieces twice (every 10 to 12 minutes), for about 35 minutes, until barely tender when pierced with a fork. Remove from the oven and keep warm.

Fill a large pot with salted water and bring to a boil for cooking the pasta. While the water heats, in a frying pan, heat the remaining 2 tablespoons oil over medium heat. Add the pancetta and cook, stirring often, for about 6 minutes, until browned and crisp. Using a slotted spoon, transfer the pancetta to a plate. Pour off all but 1 tablespoon fat from the pan and return the pan to low heat. Add the panko and toast, stirring constantly, for about 2 minutes, until lightly browned. Transfer to a small bowl.

Line a plate with paper towels. In a small frying pan, heat the remaining 1/4 cup (60 ml) oil over medium-high heat until hot. Working in batches of 6 to 8 leaves, fry the sage for 5 to 10 seconds, until crisp. Using a fork or tongs, transfer the leaves to the towel-lined plate to drain. When the last batch has been fried, turn off the heat and add the butter to the hot oil to melt. Keep warm off the heat.

Add the pasta to the boiling water and cook, stirring occasionally, according to the package directions, until al dente. Drain the pasta, reserving 1/2 cup (125 ml) of the cooking water.

Transfer the pasta to a large serving bowl, add the reserved cooking water and the oil-butter mixture, and toss to coat the pasta evenly. Add the squash, panko, pecans, parsley, and cheese and toss well again. Garnish with the fried sage leaves and serve immediately.

PENNE WITH GREENS PESTO AND ARTICHOKES

This pesto, flavored with toasted pecans and pecan oil, works well with spinach, arugula, turnip or collard greens, or nearly any other greens you choose. The pesto recipe yields twice as much as you will need for the pasta, so save the remainder for dipping raw vegetables.

PESTO

1¼ cups (143 g) chopped pecans, toasted

½ cup (75 g) pitted green olives

3 cloves garlic

½ pound (250 g) trimmed and chopped fresh greens
  (about 4 cups)

Finely grated zest and juice of 2 lemons

1 teaspoon salt

½ teaspoon freshly ground black pepper

½ cup (125 ml) pecan oil

⅓ cup (45 g) freshly grated Parmigiano-Reggiano cheese

1 pound (500 g) dried mini penne pasta

½ cup (60 g) pecan halves, toasted

2 jars (7½ ounces/235 g each) quartered
  marinated artichoke hearts, drained

Freshly grated Parmigiano-Reggiano cheese, for serving

To make the pesto, in a food processor, combine the pecans, olives, and garlic and pulse until finely chopped. Add the greens, lemon zest and juice, salt, and pepper and pulse six to eight times, until the greens are finely chopped. With the processor running, pour in the oil in a slow, steady stream. Add the Parmigiano-Reggiano and pulse several times until the sauce is smooth. You will need only 1 cup (250 g) for this

recipe. Transfer the remainder to an airtight container, top with a thin film of oil, and refrigerate for up to 3 days.

Fill a large pot with salted water and bring to a boil. Add the pasta and cook, stirring occasionally, according to the package directions, until al dente.

Drain the pasta and transfer to a large serving bowl. Add the 1 cup (250 g) pesto, pecans, and artichoke hearts and toss well. Serve immediately, with Parmigiano-Reggiano on the side.

PECANS AND PASTA

When I'm putting together a pasta dish, I often use pecans as a secret weapon. Take for instance pumpkin ravioli, one of my favorite dishes. The pumpkin ravioli will be creamy, rich, and succulent, but chopped pecans tossed with a little brown butter, sage, and wild mushrooms always provide just the correct amount of texture to take the dish over the top. Sometimes after I have tossed *tagliolini* with black trumpet mushrooms, I sprinkle just a few toasted and chopped pecans on top. They give the dish a little pop and marry beautifully with the freshly grated Parmigiano-Reggiano cheese.

—JAMES FIALA, chef and restaurateur of
The Crossing and Acero

Farro with Sautéed Kale, Shiitakes, and Pecans SERVES 8

Farro, *an ancient Italian whole grain, is a healthy alternative to everyday staples like white rice and pasta. It has a nutty flavor, a tender, chewy texture, is high in protein, and boasts a wealth of complex carbohydrates. Cooked to a near risotto-like consistency, this comforting dish, rich with mushrooms and pecans, will warm you up on the coldest winter days.*

1 ounce (30 g) dried porcini mushrooms, chopped

1½ cups (330 g) farro

2 tablespoons pecan oil

1 yellow onion, chopped

2 cloves garlic, minced

6½ ounces (200 g) kale, stemmed and chopped
    (about 3 cups)

12 ounces (340 g) fresh shiitake mushrooms,
    stemmed and caps sliced

1 tablespoon fresh thyme leaves

1 teaspoon finely grated lemon zest

½ cup (125 ml) dry white wine

5 cups (1.1 l) chicken broth

1 cup (115 g) chopped pecans, toasted

½ teaspoon salt

¼ teaspoon freshly ground black pepper

½ cup (60 g) freshly grated Parmigiano-Reggiano cheese,
    plus more for garnish

8 lemon wedges, for serving

Put the porcini in a heatproof bowl, pour in boiling water to cover, and let sit for 30 minutes, until rehydrated. Lift out the mushrooms with your fingers or a slotted spoon, avoiding any grit at the bottom of the bowl, and set aside. Put the farro into a fine-mesh sieve and rinse well under warm running water. Drain and set aside.

In a Dutch oven, heat the oil over medium heat. Add the onion and garlic and cook, stirring often, for about 5 minutes, until tender. Add the kale and cook, stirring occasionally, for 3 minutes. Add the shiitakes and cook for 2 minutes. Stir in the thyme and lemon zest and continue to cook, stirring often, for about 5 more minutes, until onion is translucent.

Add the farro and soaked porcini and cook for 1 minute, stirring constantly. Pour in the wine and cook, stirring, until the wine is absorbed. Pour in the broth, adjust the heat to maintain a simmer, cover, and cook, stirring about every 10 minutes, for 30 minutes. Add the pecans, re-cover, and continue to cook, stirring about every 10 minutes, for about 20 minutes longer, until the farro is tender and liquid is absorbed.

Season with the salt and pepper and stir in the Parmigiano-Reggiano. Serve immediately, with more cheese and the lemon wedges on the side.

Baked Acorn Squash Stuffed with Rainbow Chard, Pecans, and Herbed Barley

Acorn squash, yet another food brought to the newcomers' pantry by Native Americans, adorns many fall tables, either decoratively or as a meal! These generously overstuffed winter squashes make an ideal vegetarian main course. Topped with browned butter, pecans, and panko, they showcase many of the colors and flavors of autumn.

3 acorn squashes
½ cup (75 g) pearl barley
1½ cups (375 ml) spiced apple cider
2 tablespoons unsalted butter, plus 2 tablespoons
  unsalted butter, melted
½ sweet onion, chopped
10 rainbow chard stalks, stemmed and leaves chopped
2 tablespoons pure maple syrup
1 teaspoon cider vinegar
¾ cup (75 g) pecan halves, toasted and chopped
3 tablespoons pomegranate seeds
3 tablespoons chopped fresh flat-leaf parsley
1 tablespoon chopped fresh oregano
1 teaspoon chopped fresh thyme
1 teaspoon salt

¼ cup (30 g) pecans, toasted and chopped
¼ cup (10 g) panko bread crumbs

Preheat the oven to 400°F (200°C). Using a fork, prick each squash about ten times and place on a sheet pan. Bake for about 1 hour, until tender when pierced with a small, sharp knife and squash skin is slightly wrinkled. Remove from the oven and let the squashes cool until they can be handled.

While the squashes bake and cool slightly, cook the barley according to the package directions, then drain and set aside.

In a small saucepan, bring the apple cider to a boil and boil for 10 minutes, until reduced by about one-third and slightly syrupy. Set aside.

Cut each squash in half lengthwise and, using a spoon, scoop out and discard the seeds. Arrange the halves, hollow side up, on the work surface. If the any of the squash halves won't sit firmly upright, cut a thin slice off the rounded bottom.

In a large frying pan, melt 2 tablespoons butter over medium heat. Add the onion and cook, stirring often, for about 5 minutes, until tender. Add the chard, maple syrup, and vinegar and cook, stirring occasionally, for 2 to 3 minutes. Stir in the cooked barley, ½ cup (50 g) of the pecans, the pomegranate seeds, parsley, oregano, thyme, and salt and mix well.

Spoon the stuffing into the squash halves, dividing it evenly. Arrange the squash halves on a clean sheet pan and drizzle the reduced cider over the stuffing. In a small bowl, stir together the 2 tablespoons melted butter, panko, and the remaining ¼ cup (25 g) pecans, then divide the mixture evenly among the squash halves, spooning it over the stuffing.

Bake the squash for about 15 minutes, until topping is golden brown. Serve immediately.

Roasted Cod with Pecans and Panko

Firm, meaty cod can handle the weight of the coating of pecans and panko bound together with a little Dijon mustard. The crumb mixture seals the moisture into the fillets and creates a robust, crisp crust. Roasting the fish on parchment paper makes the fillets easy to transfer when serving. Large pieces of fish work best here. If fresh cod is not available, grouper makes a fine substitute.

1 cup (45 g) panko bread crumbs

1/2 cup (60 g) freshly grated Parmigiano-Reggiano cheese

1/4 cup (25 g) pecan halves, toasted and chopped

2 tablespoons mayonnaise

1 teaspoon Dijon mustard

1 teaspoon fresh thyme, chopped

Finely grated zest of 1 lemon

2 1/4 pounds (1.1 kg) fresh cod fillets, cut into 6 equal pieces

1 tablespoon extra-virgin olive oil

1/2 teaspoon salt

1/2 teaspoon freshly ground pepper

2 tablespoons unsalted butter, cut into small pieces

Lemon wedges, for serving

Preheat the oven to 400°F (200°C). Line a large sheet pan with parchment paper.

In a bowl, stir together the panko, cheese, pecans, mayonnaise, mustard, thyme, and lemon zest.

Arrange the fish fillets in a single layer on the prepared pan. Lightly brush the tops of the fillets with the oil. Sprinkle evenly with the salt and pepper. Divide the panko mixture evenly among the fillets, pressing it firmly on the top of each fillet. Dot the panko mixture evenly with the butter.

Bake for 12 to 14 minutes, until the fish flakes when tested with a fork. Serve immediately, with lemon wedges on the side.

Pecan-Studded Blue Crab Cakes

Blue crabs are one of the benefits of living near salt marshes on the East Coast. The claw meat is sweet and delicate. Adding pecans to the crumb coating enhances the buttery flavor of the crabmeat. Dressed with a nutty rémoulade, these crab cakes make an impressive lunch or dinner main course, served with a simple salad on the side. If you don't live in an area where blue crabs are available, choose the best crabmeat your seafood market offers. The grades of fresh crabmeat are lump, backfin, jumbo, and claw. Any of these will work, but claw meat comes in smaller pieces so it's the easiest to work into crab cakes.

PECAN RÉMOULADE

1 cup (250 ml) mayonnaise
1/4 cup (28 g) chopped pecans, toasted
1 tablespoon chopped fresh chives
2 teaspoons Dijon mustard
Juice of 1 lemon

CRAB CAKES

1 pound (500 g) fresh crabmeat, preferably from blue crabs
1 red chile, seeded and diced
2 green onions, white and light green parts, thinly sliced
1 clove garlic, minced
2 tablespoons chopped fresh chives
2 tablespoons mayonnaise
1 tablespoon Dijon mustard
Finely grated zest of 1 lemon
3/4 teaspoon salt
1/4 teaspoon freshly ground black pepper
2 large eggs, lightly beaten
1 cup (40 g) panko bread crumbs
1/2 cup (60 g) chopped pecans, toasted

4 tablespoons (60 g) unsalted butter

To make the rémoulade, combine all of the ingredients in a bowl and mix well. You should have just over 1 cup (250 ml). Cover and refrigerate until ready to serve.

To make the crab cakes, spread the crabmeat on a sheet pan. Run your fingers through the meat to find and remove any shell or cartilage fragments. Transfer the crabmeat to a bowl. Add the red chile, green onions, garlic, chives, mayonnaise, mustard, lemon zest, salt, pepper, and eggs and mix well. Fold in the panko and pecans.

To shape the crab cakes, use a 1/3-cup (80-ml) measuring cup to scoop out portions of the crabmeat mixture, flattening each scoop slightly into a cake about 2 1/2 inches (6 cm) in diameter and 1 1/4 inches (3 cm) thick. You should have 16 crab cakes. (You can wrap the uncooked cakes securely and freeze them for up to 1 month, then thaw and cook them as directed.)

Line a large plate with paper towels. In a large nonstick frying pan, melt 2 tablespoons of the butter over medium heat. Add half of the crab cakes and cook, turning once, for 3 to 4 minutes on each side, until browned. Use a small offset spatula and turn them carefully to avoid breaking them up.

Transfer the cakes to the towel-lined plate to drain. Cook the remaining cakes the same way, using the remaining 2 tablespoons butter.

Serve the crab cakes immediately, with the rémoulade on the side.

FRIED PECAN-COATED OYSTERS WITH OLD BAY RÉMOULADE

Plump, briny oysters bathed in a batter and fried until crisp are one of the classic shellfish dishes. Look for the largest oysters you can find to achieve the ideal ratio of breading to oyster. Draining on a wire rack, instead of on paper towels, ensures the entire oyster is crisp on the outside. In the South, oysters are served with grits or hushpuppies (or with both, if you're lucky).

OLD BAY RÉMOULADE
1 cup (250 ml) mayonnaise
1 tablespoon capers, drained and coarsely chopped
1 teaspoon Dijon mustard
1 tablespoon chopped fresh flat-leaf parsley
1 tablespoon Old Bay Seasoning

OYSTERS
Canola oil, for deep-frying
3 cups (470 g) all-purpose flour
1 cup (115 g) chopped pecans, finely ground
1 tablespoon baking powder
2 teaspoons kosher salt
1 teaspoon freshly ground black pepper
1 jar (1 pint/500 ml) shucked oysters, drained

Lemon wedges, for serving

To make the rémoulade, combine all of the ingredients in a bowl and mix well. You should have about 1 cup (250 ml). Cover and refrigerate until ready to serve.

To cook the oysters, in a deep fryer or large, heavy, deep pot, pour the oil to a depth of 3 inches (7.5 cm) and heat over high heat to 360°F (185°C) on a deep-frying thermometer. Set a wire rack over a sheet pan.

While the oil heats, in a bowl, whisk together the flour, pecans, baking powder, salt, and pepper. One at a time, dredge the oysters in the flour mixture, coating evenly, and set aside on a plate.

When the oil is ready, working in two or three batches, carefully lower the oysters into the oil and fry for 1 to 1½ minutes, until golden brown. Using a slotted spoon or wire skimmer, transfer the oysters to the wire rack to drain.

Serve the oysters immediately, with the rémoulade and lemon wedges on the side.

RAINBOW TROUT WITH LEMON, THYME, AND PECAN CRUST

Cold mountain streams running through northern Georgia are often brimming with rainbow trout. They are one of the easiest fish to cook and have a sweet, tender flavor. A light coating of pecan meal, herbs, and lemon zest seals in the delicate flavor, making this a main course favorite whenever fresh trout is available.

1 3/4 cups (200 g) pecan meal (page 32)
Finely grated zest and juice of 3 lemons
2 tablespoons chopped fresh thyme
4 skin-on rainbow trout fillets
3/4 teaspoon salt
1/2 teaspoon freshly ground black pepper
4 tablespoons (60 g) unsalted butter
Fresh thyme sprigs, for garnish

In a wide, shallow bowl, stir together the pecan meal, lemon zest, and thyme. Sprinkle the trout fillets on both sides with the salt and pepper. One at a time, dredge the fillets in the pecan meal mixture, coating evenly on both sides.

In a large nonstick frying pan, melt 2 tablespoons of the butter over medium-low heat. Add 2 trout fillets, skin side up, to the hot frying pan. Cook for about 4 minutes, until browned on the first side. Carefully flip the fillets and cook on the second side for about 2 minutes, until browned and the flesh just flakes when tested with a fork. Transfer the fillets to a serving platter and keep warm. Wipe out the pan with a paper towel and return to medium-low heat. Add the remaining 2 tablespoons butter to the frying pan and cook the remaining 2 fillets the same way, then transfer them to the platter.

Raise the heat to medium, add the lemon juice, and cook for 1 minute, stirring to loosen any browned bits from the bottom of the pan. Spoon the pan sauce over the trout fillets, garnish with thyme, and serve immediately.

Pecan Varieties (Carya illinoinensis), watercolor by Ellen Isham Schutt, 1907; Special Collections, USDA National Agricultural Library

Stir-Fried Pecan Kung Pao Chicken

*The most popular Chinese take-out dish can now come straight from
your own kitchen. It carries an explosion of salt, sweet, and spice in
every bite. Look for black vinegar, palm sugar, and rice wine at
Asian markets.*

Marinade

2 tablespoons soy sauce

1 tablespoon Shaoxing wine (Chinese rice wine)

1½ teaspoons cornstarch

1 pound (500 g) boneless, skinless chicken thighs,
cut into 1-inch (2.5 cm) pieces

1 tablespoon black vinegar

1 teaspoon soy sauce

1 teaspoon hoisin sauce

1 teaspoon toasted sesame oil

2 teaspoons finely chopped palm sugar

1 teaspoon cornstarch

¼ teaspoon cayenne pepper

2 tablespoons pecan oil

6 small dried chiles

4 green onions, white and light green parts, sliced,
plus more for garnish

1 clove garlic, sliced

½-inch (12-mm) piece fresh ginger, peeled and grated

½ cup (50 g) pecan halves, toasted and chopped

To make the marinade, in a small bowl, stir together the soy
sauce, wine, and cornstarch until the cornstarch dissolves.

Put the chicken into a large resealable plastic bag. Pour
the marinade into the bag, seal closed, then turn the bag a
few times to coat the chicken evenly. Refrigerate for 8 hours.

In another small bowl, combine the vinegar, soy sauce,
hoisin sauce, sesame oil, palm sugar, cornstarch, and cayenne
and whisk until the sugar and cornstarch dissolve. Set the
bowl near the stove.

Using a slotted spoon, remove the chicken from the
marinade, discarding the marinade. In a wok or large frying
pan, heat the pecan oil over medium-high heat. Add the
chiles and toast for 30 seconds to 1 minute, until lightly
browned. Add the chicken and cook, stirring frequently, for
4 minutes. Add the green onions, garlic, and ginger and cook,
stirring, for 1 minute. Add the vinegar sauce and pecans and
cook, stirring, for about 2 minutes, until the chicken is
cooked through and the sauce has thickened slightly.

Transfer to a serving bowl or platter and garnish with
green onions. Serve immediately.

PLATE CXLII

American Sparrow Hawk, FALCO SPARVERIUS, *Linn* *Male.1.Female.2.* *Butter-nut or White walnut Juglans cinerea.*

American Sparrow Hawk and Butternuts, from *The Birds of North America,* by John James Audubon, c. 1831, Boston Public Library

CHILE CHICKEN ENCHILADAS WITH PECAN MOLE

When intense spices, rich chocolate, smoky peppers, and roasted nuts intertwine, an unforgettable Mexican sauce is born. This cinnamon-laced mole, which can be used to top enchiladas and tamales or as a dip for warm tortillas, is something you will want to have on hand.

A heavy-duty blender works best for grinding the cinnamon stick and other ingredients in the mole. If you have a less powerful blender or a food processor, use 1/2 to 1 teaspoon ground cinnamon in place of the cinnamon stick and be sure to stop and scrape down the sides of the canister or bowl often.

PECAN MOLE

5 whole cloves

1 cinnamon stick

1/2 teaspoon aniseeds

1/4 teaspoon coriander seeds

1/4 cup (30 g) sesame seeds

4 tablespoons (60 ml) pecan oil

6 guajillo chiles, stemmed and seeded

4 ancho chiles, stemmed and seeded

2 (6-inch) corn tortillas, chopped into 1-inch (2.5 cm) pieces

1/4 cup (40 g) raisins

1/2 cup (50 g) pecan halves

1 white onion, chopped

2 cloves garlic

1 can (14 1/2 ounces/455 g) diced tomatoes, undrained

1 disk (2 3/4 ounces/81 g) Mexican chocolate, chopped

2 cups (500 ml) chicken broth

Sugar, as needed

Salt

Nonstick cooking spray, for the baking dish

1 tablespoon extra-virgin olive oil

1 white onion, sliced

4 cups (560 g) shredded cooked chicken

2 cups (500 g) shredded Monterey Jack cheese

1 can (4 ounces/125 g) diced green chiles, undrained

3/4 teaspoon salt

1/2 teaspoon ground cumin

14 (6-inch) corn tortillas, warmed

1/4 pound (125 g) queso fresco, crumbled

(continued next page)

To make the mole, in a large dry frying pan, toast the cloves, cinnamon, aniseeds, coriander seeds, and sesame seeds over low heat for 3 to 4 minutes, until fragrant and the seeds have begun to turn golden. Transfer to a blender.

Return the pan to medium heat and add 3 tablespoons of the pecan oil. When the oil is hot, add all of the chiles and cook, turning often, for about 3 minutes, until very fragrant. Transfer the chiles to a heatproof bowl, add boiling water to cover (at least 2 cups/500 ml), and let stand for about 30 minutes, until pliable.

Add the tortillas, raisins, and pecans to the frying pan and toast over medium heat, stirring often, for about 2 minutes, until lightly browned. Add the contents of the pan, including the oil, to the blender. Remove the chiles from their soaking water and add them to the blender. Measure 2 cups (500 ml) of the soaking water, add it to the blender, and process until the mixture is smooth.

Heat the remaining 1 tablespoon pecan oil in the same frying pan over medium heat. Add the onion and garlic and cook, stirring often, for about 5 minutes, until tender. Add the tomatoes and chocolate and cook, stirring, for about 5 minutes, until the chocolate melts. Add the broth and continue to cook, stirring occasionally, for 5 minutes to blend the flavors.

Pour the chocolate mixture into the blender holding the chile mixture. Beginning at low speed and gradually moving to high speed, process until the sauce is smooth. Return the sauce to the frying pan and cook over medium-low heat, stirring often, for about 20 minutes, until thickened. Taste and adjust with sugar and salt as needed. You should have about 6 cups (1.5 l) mole. You will need 2½ cups (625 ml) of the sauce for this recipe. The remainder will keep in an airtight container in the refrigerator for up to 5 days or in the freezer for up to 2 months.

Preheat the oven to 350°F (180°C). Spray a 13-by-9-inch (33-by-23-cm) baking dish with cooking spray. Spread ½ cup (125 ml) of the mole on the bottom of the dish.

In a frying pan, heat the olive oil over medium heat. Add the onion and cook, stirring occasionally, for about 5 minutes, until tender. Transfer to a large bowl. Add the chicken, Monterey Jack cheese, green chiles, salt, cumin, and ¾ cup (180 ml) of the mole to the onion and mix well.

Spoon about ⅓ cup (80 ml) of the filling along the center of each warm tortilla, then roll up the tortilla around the filling and place seam side down in the prepared baking dish. Spoon the remaining 1¼ cups (310 ml) mole over the enchiladas.

Bake the enchiladas for about 25 minutes, until the edges of the tortillas are browned. Remove from the oven, sprinkle the queso fresco evenly over the top, and serve hot.

Right: (top to bottom) Mexico is the second largest pecan producer in the world. Pecans are sold in local markets such as those at the Central Mercado de Abastos in Oaxaca City, and are a popular ingredient in traditional moles.
Far right: Anna and Allison Millican pick pecans in their family orchard.

NUEZ
QUEBRADA

NUEZ
EN MITADES

MAIZ
POZOLERO

When I was a child, my grandmother owned an estate on the outskirts of Guatemala City. A huge pecan tree that she had ordered from the United States and planted in the mid-1950s stood at the entrance of the long, winding driveway. Always enamored of food, I soon discovered the edible oval-shaped beauties under the tree, using rocks to crack them open to savor their sweet flesh. My brothers then carved a "V" at the top of a very long branch so I could get the pecans from the tall limbs without having to climb the tree.

To this day, I love eating pecans from the shell and enjoy adding them to my new southern–Latino dishes, such as Cajeta and Bourbon Bread Pudding, or my famous Pecan Cookies with Guatemalan Coffee Granita.

—Sandra A. Gutierrez, culinary instructor and author of *The New Southern-Latino Table* and *Empanadas: The Hand-Held Pies of Latin America*

GLAZED DUCK BREAST WITH APRICOTS AND PECANS

A glimmering pecan-studded glaze is the finishing touch to this succulent Asian-inspired main course. Duck breasts are usually sold frozen and should always come with the skin attached, beneath which is a generous layer of fat. Do not be tempted to remove the skin and fat, as they are the best part! Gently scoring the skin allows the fat to render, so no cooking oil is needed in the frying pan. Turn on your exhaust hood and have a splatter screen nearby, as searing the skin can cause a little smoke to rise and droplets of grease to fly.

DUCK AND MARINADE

4 skin-on boneless duck breasts, about 1/2 pound
    (250 g) each
1/2 cup (125 ml) rice vinegar
1/4 cup (60 ml) soy sauce
1/4 cup (60 ml) extra-virgin olive oil
1 shallot, thinly sliced

GLAZE

3/4 cup (240 g) apricot preserves
1/4 cup (25 g) pecan halves, toasted and chopped
1 1/2 tablespoons rice vinegar
1 tablespoon soy sauce
2 teaspoons extra-virgin olive oil
1/8 teaspoon salt

Pat the duck breasts dry with paper towels. With a sharp knife, cut 6 evenly spaced diagonal slashes in the skin and fat on each breast half, being careful not to cut into the flesh.

To make the marinade, combine vinegar, soy sauce, oil, and shallot in a large resealable plastic bag. Add the duck breasts, seal the bag closed, and then turn the bag a few times to coat the duck evenly. Refrigerate the duck for 45 minutes. After 30 minutes, preheat the oven to 350°F (180°C).

To make the glaze, combine all of the ingredients in a small saucepan over low heat. Bring to a simmer, stirring often, and then simmer, stirring occasionally, for 5 minutes to blend the flavors. Turn off the heat and keep warm.

To cook the duck breasts, heat a large heavy frying pan (do not use non-stick) over medium heat. When the pan is hot, add 2 duck breasts, skin side down, and cook for 3 minutes without disturbing them. Turn the breasts over, spoon about 1 tablespoon of the glaze over each breast, and cook for 1 minute longer. Transfer the breasts, skin side up, to a sheet pan and spoon 1 tablespoon glaze on top of each breast. Wipe out the pan with a paper towel and return to medium heat. Cook the remaining 2 duck breasts the same way and add them to the sheet pan.

Roast the duck breasts for 6 to 8 minutes, until an instant-read thermometer inserted into the thickest part of a breast registers 135°F (57°C) for medium-rare. Transfer the duck breasts to a cutting board and let rest for 10 minutes.

Slice each breast across the grain into 6 thick slices and transfer to a warmed serving platter or individual plates. Spoon the remaining glaze over the duck and serve immediately.

TEXAS-SIZE PECAN ANDOUILLE BURGERS WITH COWBOY SAUCE

It's unexpected to bite into a burger and find the delightful texture of pecans and the heat of andouille sausage. If you prefer a smaller serving size, shape the beef into 12 patties and grill for about 4 minutes on each side. Little brioche buns are perfect for these sliders.

COWBOY SAUCE

1 cup (250 ml) mayonnaise

1 1/2 tablespoons adobo sauce from canned chipotle chiles in adobo sauce

1 1/2 tablespoons A.1. Sauce

BURGERS

2 pounds (1 kg) ground chuck

2 cups (230 g) chopped pecans, toasted

14 ounces (440 g) andouille sausage, cut into 1/4-inch (6-mm) pieces

8 slices extra-sharp Cheddar cheese

8 large hamburger buns

1 large sweet onion, sliced into rings

To make the sauce, combine all of the ingredients in a small bowl and mix well. Cover and refrigerate until serving or for up to 3 days.

To make the burgers, prepare a medium fire (350°F/180°C) in a charcoal or gas grill.

In a large bowl, combine the chuck, pecans, and andouille and mix with your hands until all of the ingredients are evenly distributed. Divide into eight equal portions and shape each portion into a patty about 4 1/2 inches (11.5 cm) in diameter. Make a shallow indentation in the center of each patty to prevent the patties from puffing up in the center during cooking.

Place the patties on the cooking grate, close the grill lid, and grill for 8 minutes on the first side. Flip the patties over, close the grill lid again, and cook for about 5 minutes on the second side, adding a slice of cheese to each patty after 4 minutes, until the patties are no longer pink in the center when tested with a knife tip. Transfer the patties to a platter and let rest for 5 minutes before serving.

Slather the cut sides of each bun with the sauce. Top each bun bottom with a burger and onion rings and close with the bun top. Serve immediately.

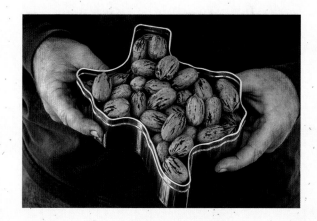

Desserts

Classic Pecan Pie

Pecan pies have been dressed up in countless ways—with bourbon and dark chocolate to name just two—but the classic never goes out of style. Even so, there's still room for differences. Wherever there is an oven in the South, you'll find a debate about the proper way to add pecans to pies: halves or chopped? The solution? Make it both ways and decide which one you like best.

CRUST

1 1/3 cups (215 g) all-purpose flour, plus more
    for the work surface

1/2 teaspoon salt

1/2 cup (125 g) vegetable shortening

4 to 6 tablespoons (60 to 90 ml) ice water

FILLING

1 1/3 cups (153 g) pecans (chopped or halves)

1 cup (220 g) firmly packed light brown sugar

1 cup (315 ml) light corn syrup

4 large eggs, lightly beaten

4 tablespoons unsalted butter, melted

1 1/2 teaspoons pure vanilla extract

1/4 teaspoon salt

Softly whipped cream, for serving (optional)

To make the crust, in a bowl, stir together the flour and salt. Using a pastry blender or two knives, cut the shortening into the flour mixture until the mixture forms coarse crumbs the size of small peas. Sprinkle 4 tablespoons (60 ml) of the ice water over the flour-shortening mixture and stir and toss with a fork just until evenly moistened. If the dough seems too crumbly, add a little more ice water. Gather the dough together and shape into a ball. Wrap in plastic wrap and chill for 45 minutes.

Preheat the oven to 450°F (230°C).

Lightly flour a work surface and transfer the dough to it. Roll out the dough into a round 11 to 12 inches (28 to 30 cm) in diameter and 1/8 inch (3 mm) thick. Carefully roll the dough around the rolling pin and position the pin over a 9-inch (23-cm) pie dish. Unroll the dough, centering it in the dish, and gently press it onto the bottom and up the sides. Trim off the excess dough, leaving a 3/4-inch (2 cm) overhang. Fold the overhang under and crimp the edges.

Line the crust with a piece of aluminum foil or parchment paper and fill with pie weights or dried beans. Bake the crust for 3 minutes. Remove the weights and foil, return the crust to the oven, and bake for 3 minutes longer. Transfer to a wire rack and let cool. Reduce the oven temperature to 325°F (165°C).

To make the filling, combine all of the ingredients in a bowl and stir to mix well. Pour into the cooled pie crust.

Bake for about 55 minutes, until the filling is set and pecans are deeply browned and the crust is golden. Tent the pie with foil if the crust begins to get too dark before the pie is ready. Let cool completely (about 1 hour) on a rack before serving. Serve with softly whipped cream, if desired.

Mexican Dark Chocolate Pecan Shortbread Tart

Inspired by traditional cinnamon-spiced Mexican hot cocoa, the filling of this impressive tart is chocolate as dark as midnight mixed with the heat of cayenne pepper. After baking, a reflective shine, like that of a fine ganache, can be admired from across the room. If the tart is refrigerated, the sheen fades away. Top with coarsely chopped toasted pecans before serving.

TART SHELL

2 cups (315 g) all-purpose flour

1/8 teaspoon salt

1 cup (250 g) unsalted butter, at room temperature

1/2 cup (60 g) powdered sugar

2/3 cup (77 g) finely chopped pecans, toasted

FILLING

1 cup (250 ml) heavy cream

1/2 cup (125 ml) whole milk

10 ounces (315 g) dark chocolate (72 percent cacao), chopped

2 tablespoons granulated sugar

1 teaspoon ground cinnamon

1/4 teaspoon salt

1/4 teaspoon cayenne pepper

2 large eggs, beaten

1/2 teaspoon pure almond extract

1/2 cup (58 g) coarsely chopped pecans, toasted, for garnish

Preheat the oven to 350°F (180°C).

To make the tart shell, in a medium bowl, stir together the flour and salt. In a large bowl, using a handheld mixer, beat the butter on medium speed for about 1 minute, until creamy. Add the powdered sugar and continue to beat on medium speed until thoroughly combined. On low speed, gradually add the flour mixture and continue to beat until the mixture is no longer crumbly and starts to come together into a ball. Stir in the pecans, mixing just until evenly distributed.

Lightly dust a work surface with flour. Gather the dough together, transfer to the floured surface, and form into a large disk. Place the disk on the bottom of a 9-inch (23-cm) fluted tart pan with a removable bottom, then press the dough evenly onto the bottom and up the sides of the pan. Cover and chill for 20 minutes.

Transfer the chilled crust to a sheet pan. Line the crust with a piece of aluminum foil or parchment paper and fill with pie weights or dried beans. Bake the crust for 15 minutes. Remove the weights and foil, return the tart shell to the oven, and bake for 5 minutes longer. Let cool completely on a wire rack. Lower the oven temperature to 325°F (165°C).

(continued next page)

Mexican Dark Chocolate Pecan Shortbread Tart (continued)

To make the filling, in a saucepan, combine the cream and milk and heat over medium-low heat just until the mixture begins to bubble around the edges of the pan. Remove from the heat. Add the chocolate and stir until melted. Add the granulated sugar, cinnamon, salt, and cayenne and whisk until blended. Then whisk in the eggs and almond extract, mixing thoroughly. Pour the filling into the cooled tart shell.

Bake for 15 to 20 minutes, until the filling is set and the surface is glossy. Transfer to a wire rack and garnish the top with the pecans. Let cool completely, then slip the tart free of the pan ring and carefully slide it off the pan base onto a serving plate to serve.

CHOCOLATE MOUSSE AND PECAN BUTTER PARFAITS

Rich, fluffy chocolate mousse meets creamy pecan butter in this
perfectly decadent parfait. It is the best of both worlds for chocoholics
and pecan fanatics. Making this dessert uses more mixing bowls than
most recipes, so be sure you have three bowls ready before you begin.
Serve in parfait glasses for a table dessert or in ½-pint (250-ml) jars
with lids for toting (packed into a cooler) to a picnic or ballgame.

1 package (9 ounces/270 g) chocolate wafers
  (such as Nabisco Famous Chocolate Wafers)
3 tablespoons unsalted butter, melted
1 cup (250 ml) heavy cream
2 tablespoons powdered sugar
1½ teaspoons pure vanilla extract
¾ cup (233 g) pecan butter (page 33)
1 can (14 ounces/440 g) sweetened condensed milk
3½ ounces (105 g) dark chocolate (72% cacao), chopped
Toasted chopped pecans, for garnish

Remove half of the wafers from the package and reserve the remaining half for another use. Break up the chocolate wafers into a food processor and pulse until finely ground. Add the butter and pulse until the crumbs are evenly moistened.

Divide the crumb mixture evenly among eight ½-cup (125-ml) parfait glasses or jars (about 1 tablespoon per container) and press evenly over the bottom.

In a bowl, combine the cream, powdered sugar, and ½ teaspoon of the vanilla. Using a handheld mixer, beat on medium-high speed until stiff peaks form.

In another bowl, combine the pecan butter, half of the sweetened condensed milk, and ½ teaspoon of the vanilla and mix well. Whisk in half of the whipped cream. Set aside.

Combine the chocolate and the remaining ½ teaspoon vanilla in a heatproof bowl. Set the bowl over (not touching) gently simmering water in a saucepan and heat, stirring constantly, until the chocolate melts. Remove the bowl from the saucepan. Whisk the remaining sweetened condensed milk into the melted chocolate, mixing well. Then fold in the remaining whipped cream just until combined.

Divide the pecan butter mixture evenly among the glasses or jars, spooning it on top of the crust. Top with the chocolate mixture, again dividing evenly. Refrigerate, uncovered, for at least 4 hours or up to 1 day. Garnish with pecans before serving.

A NOSE FOR NUTS

In Atlanta, I know the pecans are falling when I feel a certain telltale tug on my dog's leash. The minute my neighborhood's random trees un-clench their fists to drop the season's first fruit onto the sidewalk, Shirley comes to a full stop. She wants a snack.

At such moments, I can't help but take pity on my short-legged, sausage-shaped dachs-hund–shih tzu mix as she tussles with a half-open pecan. I bend over, retrieve her treasure, sort the buttery nutmeat from the bitter shell, and share it with my pecan-loving girl. Taking a nibble myself, my mind goes dancing back to my south Georgia childhood.

Gathering pecans on the family farm, I could never resist an impromptu breakfast. Most of the nuts I collected made their way into my mother and grandmother's holiday goodies. My job was to press one perfect half into each ball of their snowy-white divinity.

Should I ever encounter a stash of that heavenly confection, it will only take a second before a familiar nose moves in for a sniff. Dog-gone it! I have no say in the matter—half for me, half for Shirl.

—WENDELL BROCK, James Beard award-
winning food writer

Espresso Chocolate Pecan Bars

Pecans have been a part of brownie recipes forever, but these fudgy bars are extravagant, and the addition of espresso and Dutch process cocoa powder intensifies the decadence! Watch the cooking time closely. If a slightly gooey texture is desired, bake as directed. For a firmer texture, bake for a few minutes longer.

Nonstick cooking spray, for the baking pan
1/4 cup (45 g) semisweet chocolate chips
3/4 cup (185 g) unsalted butter
3/4 cup (65 g) Dutch process cocoa powder
1 1/2 cups (300 g) sugar
3 large eggs
1 cup (155 g) all-purpose flour
2 teaspoons ground espresso-roast coffee
1 teaspoon pure vanilla extract
1/8 teaspoon salt
1/2 cup (58 g) chopped pecans

Preheat the oven to 350°F (180°C). Lightly spray a 9-inch (23-cm) square baking pan with cooking spray. Line the bottom and sides of the pan with aluminum foil, allowing 2 to 3 inches (5 to 7.5 cm) to extend over the sides. Lightly spray the foil with cooking spray.

In a saucepan, combine the chocolate chips and butter over medium heat and heat, stirring constantly, for about 4 minutes, until melted. Remove from the heat and let cool for 1 minute. Whisk in the cocoa powder and sugar, mixing until blended. Whisk in the eggs, one at a time, whisking just until blended after each addition. Whisk in the flour, coffee, vanilla, and salt until fully blended. Fold in the pecans. Pour the batter into the prepared pan.

Bake for 36 to 38 minutes, until the edges just pull away from the pan. Let cool completely in the pan on a wire rack (about 30 minutes). Using the foil overhang as handles, lift the brownies from the pan and cut into eighteen 1-by-4-inch (2.5-by-10-cm) bars.

The bars will keep in an airtight container at room temperature for up to 2 days.

CLASSIC MEXICAN WEDDING COOKIES

The origin of these melt-in-your-mouth cookies is widely debated among food historians. Russia, Mexico, and Spain all claim them as native confections. Each national version has the same finishing touch, however: after baking, the nut-and-butter cookies are rolled in powdered sugar. They're served as Christmas tea cakes in Russia and given as wedding favors in Mexico. In Spain, they're spruced up with anise flavoring. No matter their country of origin, each one is a little bite of cloud-like perfection.

1 cup (250 g) unsalted butter, at room temperature

1/2 teaspoon pure vanilla extract

1/2 cup (65 g) powdered sugar, sifted, plus 1/2 cup (65 g), for dusting cookies

2 cups (315 g) all-purpose flour

3/4 cup (75 g) pecan halves, finely chopped

1/2 teaspoon salt

In a bowl, using a handheld mixer, beat together the butter and vanilla on medium speed for about 1 minute, until creamy. Gradually add the sifted powdered sugar, beating well. On low speed, add the flour, pecans, and salt and beat until blended. Cover the bowl and chill the dough for 30 minutes.

Preheat the oven to 350°F (180°C). Line a large sheet pan with parchment paper.

Scoop up the dough by the heaping tablespoon and shape into 1 1/4-inch (3-cm) balls, rolling them between your palms. Place on the prepared sheet pan, spacing them 1 inch (2.5 cm) apart.

Bake for about 18 minutes, until the bottoms are golden (the tops will be pale). Just before they are ready, place the remaining 1/2 cup (65 g) powdered sugar in a bowl. Remove the cookies from the oven and immediately roll each cookie in the sugar, coating evenly, then place on a wire rack and let cool completely (about 30 minutes).

The cookies will keep in an airtight container at room temperature for up to 4 days.

Right: Classic Mexican Wedding Cookies and Pecan Pralines (recipe page 142).

I have always loved receiving Georgia pecans as a gift, but the dilemma of what to make with them sets in as soon as the bow is untied. Pecans in the shell, perhaps picked up by a grandparent in the yard with a rolling nut picker-upper, are an offering that keeps on giving. Sitting around the table and cracking pecans is as much of a southern pastime as shelling peas on the porch is.

Even chopped pecans and small bits are a welcome gift, as they beckon to be added to salads and to toppings for casseroles or transformed into southern sweets like brittles and pralines. At Christmastime, cooks throughout the South melt sugar to dress up their pecans. For us, we've found Christmas pralines offer a sweetness that will linger in your mouth long after the candy is gone.

—Nathalie Dupree, author of three
James Beard award-winning cookbooks
including *Mastering the Art of Southern Cooking*

Pecan Pralines Makes 24 pralines

Praline recipes vary throughout the South, and Nathalie Dupree, the grande dame of southern cooking, has mastered them all. This is her version of pecan pralines and you'll agree it is one of the finest. For the best result, make this irresistible confection when the weather is dry and sunny. If it's too humid outside, the pralines will weep (and so will you).

4 tablespoons unsalted butter, plus 1 tablespoon, melted, for the pan
2 cups (400 g) sugar
1/2 cup (125 ml) light corn syrup
1/2 cup (125 ml) water
2 cups (200 g) pecan halves
1 tablespoon pure vanilla extract

Grease a sheet pan with the 1 tablespoon butter.

In a heavy saucepan, combine the sugar, corn syrup, water, and pecans and heat over low heat, stirring until the sugar dissolves. Bring the mixture to a boil, stirring occasionally, and boil until it registers 240°F (115°C) on a deep-frying thermometer (soft-ball stage). Remove from the heat, add the 4 tablespoons butter and the vanilla, and stir well to incorporate. Let cool to room temperature.

Using a handheld mixer, whip the mixture on high speed until it gradually becomes opaque and creamy. Drop by the tablespoonful onto the prepared pan and let stand at room temperature until fully set.

The pralines will keep in an airtight container at room temperature for up to 1 week.

Maple and Pecan Bread Pudding

Bread pudding is the ultimate comfort food, and this one, with the flavors of autumn, is not overly sweet, so it's a great choice for a brunch menu, too. Using bread that is a couple of days old helps every morsel absorb as much flavor as possible. If you have only fresh bread, first toast the cubes in the oven for a few minutes. Capping each serving with a dollop of liqueur-flavored whipped cream dresses up this rustic dish.

4 tablespoons unsalted butter, melted, plus more
    for the baking dish

2 cups (500 ml) half-and-half

4 large eggs

1/2 cup (58 g) chopped pecans

1/3 cup (65 g) granulated sugar

1/4 cup (85 g) pure maple syrup

1/2 teaspoon pure vanilla extract

1/8 teaspoon salt

1 loaf (1 pound/500 g) challah or brioche, 2 days old,
    cut into 1-inch (2.5-cm) cubes

Irish Whipped Cream

1 1/2 cups (375 ml) heavy cream

3 tablespoons Irish cream liqueur

2 teaspoons powdered sugar

1/2 teaspoon pure vanilla extract

Preheat the oven to 350°F (180°C). Lightly grease a 7-by-11-by-2-inch (18-by-28-by-5-cm) baking dish with butter.

In a large bowl, whisk together the half-and-half and eggs, mixing well. Add the pecans, sugar, maple syrup, melted butter, vanilla, and salt and whisk until well blended. Add the bread cubes, stir to moisten evenly, and let stand for 10 minutes.

Transfer the pudding mixture to the prepared baking dish. Bake for 45 minutes, until puffed and golden.

While the pudding bakes, make the whipped cream. In a bowl, using a handheld mixer, whip the cream on medium-high speed until soft peaks start to form. Add the liqueur, powdered sugar, and vanilla and continue to beat until stiff peaks form. Cover and refrigerate until ready to serve.

Serve the pudding warm from the oven on individual dessert plates. Top each serving with a large dollop of the whipped cream.

Mockingbird with Pecans, drawing © by Maggie Robertson, 2015

GINGER-PECAN MUESLI COOKIES

This European-inspired cookie is perfect for teatime or a cookie sampler on a dessert buffet. Make it a little bigger and you'll have a trendy "breakfast cookie" that's a healthful substitute for a muffin. Flattening the balls of dough with the bottom of a drinking glass makes the cookies easier to stack and store.

1 cup (115 g) chopped pecans
2 cups (315 g) all-purpose flour
2/3 cup (155 g) firmly packed dark brown sugar
1/2 teaspoon salt
1/2 cup (125 g) salted butter, melted and cooled
2 large eggs, at room temperature, lightly beaten
1 teaspoon pure vanilla extract
1/2 cup (50 g) muesli
1/3 cup (60 g) chopped crystallized ginger
1/4 cup (30 g) shredded unsweetened dried coconut, lightly toasted

Preheat the oven to 375°F (190°C). Line a sheet pan with parchment paper.

In a food processor, pulse 1/2 cup (60 g) of the pecans until reduced to a finely ground meal. Transfer to a bowl, add the flour, sugar, and salt, and stir to mix well.

In a second bowl, whisk together the butter, eggs, and vanilla, mixing well. Stir the butter mixture into the flour mixture, mixing until the dry ingredients are evenly moistened. Fold in the remaining 1/2 cup (65 g) chopped pecans, the muesli, ginger, and coconut.

Using an ice cream scoop or spoon, scoop up the dough and shape into golf ball–size balls, rolling them between your palms. Place on the prepared pan, spacing them 3 inches (7.5 cm) apart. Using a drinking glass or jar, flatten each dough ball into a round 1½ inches (4 cm) in diameter and ¼ inch (6 mm) thick.

Bake for about 13 minutes, until browned and sturdy. Transfer the cookies to a wire rack and let cool completely.

The cookies will keep in an airtight container at room temperature for up to 1 week or in the refrigerator for up to 1 month.

PECAN STATE

My home state of Georgia may be called The Peach State, but it's actually the number-one producer of pecans in the nation! Picking up pecans in the fall from my grandparents' yard was a big part of my childhood. My sister and I would crawl about to fill our grocery bags, the knees of our jeans damp from the wet earth. My grandmother had a tool that looked like an orange Slinky on a rod. She'd bounce the end on the ground and it would "catch" the pecans. My grandfather would take our harvest and crack them with a nutcracker he'd attached to a two-by-four. With the board bridging two chairs on the back porch, he'd place a bucket underneath and then sit in one of the chairs. Methodically, he'd reach into his sack of pecans and—whack, whack—he'd pull the handle and the shells would shatter. We'd then clean and freeze the nuts to use in cakes, pies, and cookies. I no longer harvest my own, but without fail, every autumn I buy a large amount of freshly harvested pecans to use over the course of the year.

—Virginia Willis, chef and author of *Secrets of the Southern Table* and the James Beard award-winning cookbook *Lighten Up, Y'all*

DOUBLE-PECAN CARROT CAKE WITH CREAM CHEESE FROSTING

This is a moist, dense layer cake packed with carrots and pecans, stacked high, and half-dressed with snow-white frosting. The deliciously sweet cream cheese frosting, which is spread on the top of each layer, balances the flavors of the cake perfectly. Use just a dab of frosting between the cake stand and the first layer to prevent the cake from slipping. Grating carrots by hand makes a huge difference in baked goods, so avoid the packaged shredded carrots that have often lost a lot of their natural moisture.

If you're in the mood for cupcakes, pour the batter into 30 muffin cups lined with paper liners, filling each one about two-thirds full. Bake for about 25 minutes, until they test done, and frost when cooled.

CAKE

Unsalted butter, for the cake pans

2 cups (315 g) unbleached all-purpose flour, plus more for the pans

2 cups (400 g) granulated sugar

2 teaspoons baking powder

2 teaspoons baking soda

1 1/2 teaspoons ground cinnamon

1/4 teaspoon ground cardamom

1 1/2 teaspoons salt

1 1/2 cups (375 ml) vegetable oil

4 large eggs

1 teaspoon pure vanilla extract

3/4 pound (375 g) unpeeled carrots, grated (3 cups grated)

1 cup (100 g) pecan halves, toasted and chopped

FROSTING

1 package (8 ounces/250 g) cream cheese, at room temperature

1 cup (250 g) unsalted butter, at room temperature

2 teaspoons pure vanilla extract

1/4 teaspoon salt

1 package (2 pounds/1 kg) powdered sugar

2/3 cup (67 g) pecan halves, toasted and coarsely chopped, for decorating

To make the cake, preheat the oven to 350°F (180°C). Grease three 8-inch (20-cm) round cake pans with butter, then dust with flour, tapping out the excess.

In a bowl, whisk together the flour, granulated sugar, baking powder, baking soda, cinnamon, cardamom, and salt.

In a stand mixer fitted with the paddle attachment, beat together the oil and eggs on medium speed for about 2 minutes, until well blended. Slowly add the flour mixture and mix for 2 minutes longer, until all ingredients are incorporated into the batter. With a rubber spatula, stir in the vanilla, carrots, and pecans just until incorporated. Divide the batter evenly among the prepared pans.

(continued next page)

Double-Pecan Carrot Cake (continued)

Bake the cake layers for about 30 minutes, until a toothpick inserted into the center of each layer comes out clean. Transfer to wire racks and let cool in the pans for 10 minutes. Run a thin knife blade around the inside edge of each pan to loosen the cake sides, then invert the pans onto racks, lift off the pans, and turn the layers right side up. Let cool completely.

While the cake layers are cooling, make the frosting. In the stand mixer fitted with the paddle attachment, beat together the cream cheese, butter, vanilla, and salt on low speed until smooth and creamy. Slowly add the powdered sugar, continuing to beat on low speed until thoroughly incorporated.

To assemble the cake, transfer a cake layer to a serving plate. Scoop one-third of the frosting on top and, using an icing knife or offset spatula, spread evenly to the edges. Repeat with the remaining 2 cake layers, ending with a thick layer of frosting on the top layer. Arrange the pecans in a circle on the top of the cake.

The cake can be covered and stored at room temperature until ready to serve for up to 2 days in cool weather (70°F/21°C and below). In warmer climates, cover and store in the refrigerator for up to 2 days, then bring to room temperature before serving.

AGED BALSAMIC–MACERATED CHERRY SUNDAES WITH PECAN BRITTLE

These sophisticated sundaes are best with fresh summer cherries, though thawed frozen sweet dark cherries can be substituted. Slightly thick and syrupy, aged balsamic vinegar enhances the natural sweetness in the cherries and adds a nice touch of tartness to the ice cream. The pecan brittle can be broken into larger pieces and served alone as candy. Make a double recipe of brittle and save half for later!

1½ pounds (750 g) cherries, pitted
1¼ cups (250 g) sugar
2 tablespoons aged balsamic vinegar
½ teaspoon pure vanilla extract
½ teaspoon salt
¾ cup (86 g) chopped pecans, toasted
1½ quarts (1.5 l) vanilla bean ice cream

In a nonreactive bowl, combine the cherries, ¼ cup (50 g) of the sugar, the vinegar, and vanilla and stir to coat the cherries evenly. Let stand for 2 hours, stirring about every 30 minutes.

Meanwhile, make the pecan brittle. Line a sheet pan with parchment paper. In a nonreactive frying pan, stir together the remaining 1 cup (200 g) sugar and the salt, then place over medium heat and warm, without stirring, until the sugar begins to melt. When about half of the sugar has melted, stir with a fork for about 2 minutes, until golden brown and completely melted.

Remove from the heat and immediately stir in the pecans. Quickly pour onto the prepared sheet pan and, using the back of a spoon, spread into a thin layer. Let cool for about 10 minutes, until fully set. Then, using a rolling pin or kitchen mallet, break into small pieces. (The brittle can be stored in an airtight container at room temperature for up to 4 days or in the refrigerator for up to 1 month.)

Divide the cherries and their marinating liquid evenly among individual serving dishes and top with a scoop of ice cream. Scatter the brittle over the ice cream and serve.

Still Life–Strawberries, Nuts, &c., by Raphaelle Peale, c. 1822, Art Institute of Chicago

PECAN HARVEST RESCUE

My Grandma Hill was a frugal, practical woman who valued pecans. So when something like nuts, a fatty foraged delicacy, fell from tall trees in late fall, it was truly special. Pecans dropped from trees for about a month each year, and every pecan that wasn't picked up lay in danger of getting squashed, toted away by a squirrel, or infested by a worm. That's why my mom and her siblings were up at the crack of dawn rescuing pecans from the dirt road before the school bus or farm trucks rushed through and crushed them. And that's why 'til the day Grandma Hill died, nobody pulled a car into her driveway between October and early December. Her driveway sat under a vast pecan tree whose roots had pushed through and split the concrete the way the Incredible Hulk's arms split his shirt.

But I am not frugal. I'm gonna blame it on my generation, or maybe on my parents' desire for me to have more than they had. All I know is that I didn't get the frugal gene. I wish I had. When no one's looking, I crush pecans in the driveway.

—Vivian Howard, chef and co-owner of Chef & the Farmer restaurant, award-winning author of *Deep Run Roots*, and television host of *A Chef's Life* (PBS)

Butter Pecan Ice Cream with Grilled Georgia Peaches

Georgia is blessed with two plentiful orchard crops that complement each other perfectly. It's hard to find a combination of peaches and pecans that's not irresistible. Homemade ice cream brings back sweet memories of summer for almost everyone. This ice cream is so luxurious that it's reminiscent of gelato. Be sure to wait to add the pecans to the ice cream maker late in the churning time. That way they will stay suspended in the whole batch and not sink to the bottom.

Butter Pecan Ice Cream

1 cup (220 g) firmly packed light brown sugar

3 tablespoons unsalted butter, plus 1 tablespoon, melted

1 tablespoon pure vanilla extract

1½ cups (375 ml) heavy cream

2 cups (500 ml) half-and-half

6 large egg yolks

⅔ cup (77 g) chopped pecans

⅛ teaspoon salt

Peaches

Vegetable oil, for grill cooking grate

4 large peaches

¼ cup (60 g) firmly packed light brown sugar

To make the ice cream, in a small saucepan, combine the sugar and the 3 tablespoons butter over medium-low heat and stir until the mixture looks like wet beach sand and begins to bubble. Remove from the heat and slowly whisk in the vanilla and ½ cup (125 ml) of the heavy cream. Set aside.

In a medium saucepan, whisk together the remaining 1 cup (250 ml) heavy cream and the half-and-half and heat over medium-low heat, whisking often, just until the mixture begins to bubble around the edges of the pan. Meanwhile, in a bowl, beat the egg yolks until blended. Remove the hot cream mixture from the heat and add about ¼ cup (60 ml) of it to the yolks while whisking constantly. Then pour the yolk mixture into the remaining cream mixture while whisking constantly. Return the pan to low heat and whisk the contents for about 5 minutes, until it coats the back of a spoon. Remove from the heat.

Pour the cream mixture through a fine-mesh sieve into a bowl and whisk in the reserved sugar mixture until the sugar dissolves. Cover and refrigerate the custard for at least 3 hours or up to 24 hours.

Meanwhile, preheat the oven to 350°F (180°C). On a small sheet pan, toss the pecans with the remaining 1 tablespoon melted butter and the salt, coating evenly, then spread the nuts in a single layer on the pan. Bake for about 8 minutes, until lightly browned. Pour onto a plate and let cool completely. Cover and refrigerate until needed.

(continued next page)

Butter Pecan Ice Cream with Grilled Georgia Peaches (continued)

Freeze the custard in an ice cream maker according to the manufacturer's instructions. A few minutes before the ice cream is ready, drop the reserved pecans into the ice cream maker as it continues to churn. You should have about 1 quart (1 l) ice cream. Transfer it to an airtight container and place in the freezer until serving.

When ready to serve with the peaches, prepare a medium fire (350°F/180°C) in a charcoal or gas grill. Lightly brush the cooking grate with oil to prevent sticking.

Cut each peach in half and remove and discard the pits. Place the peach halves, cut side down, on the cooking grate and grill, turning once, for about 3 minutes on each side, until softened and seared with grill marks. Transfer to a large plate and keep warm.

Put the sugar in a bowl and, one or two at a time, gently toss the hot peach halves in the sugar, coating them evenly. Return the peaches to the platter and let stand for 5 minutes.

To serve, put 2 scoops of ice cream in each individual bowl. Set a warm peach half, whole or cut into slices, alongside the ice cream and serve immediately.

INDEX

ACKNOWLEDGMENTS

Several years ago, when we were working on *Almonds: Recipes, History, Culture*, Gene and Evie Williams, of Nilo Plantation, urged us to consider making a book about pecans. Barbara has known and loved the Williams family for almost fifty years. The origins of this book are rooted in their concept and history of pecan farming. A special thanks to Ted Williams for being a part of our project.

We are delighted to have had the opportunity to collaborate once again with the talented cookbook packager Jenny Barry. Her design, wisdom, and humor, together with Bob Holmes' gorgeous photographs, gave life to these pages. Many thanks to Andrea Johnson for assisting Bob in creating the amazing photographs. Together with Bob we extend bushels full of thanks to Glenn and June Paschal for free rein at Nilo Plantation, as well as to Pearson Farm, Millican Pecan Company, and Jeffreys Ranch Pecans, who opened their doors to him for stunning location photography. We're grateful to food stylist Kim Kissling for helping to make each recipe look as delicious as it tastes and for opening her home to the photo shoot and letting us feast at her table. Writer Toni Jones tirelessly helped scout for the beautiful magnolia blossoms featured in the photography, and blessings to her neighbor Rich Miller for letting us cut blossoms from his tree.

This book has as its foundation Rebecca Lang's recipes, which sing along with her wonderful Georgia accent. She has lovingly shared her kitchen skills to celebrate the pecan in all its splendor and deliciousness. She also kindly introduced this book to her circle of southern food authors and mentors; their eagerness to conjure up pecan memories speaks to Rebecca's wide company of culinary friends and fans.

Our local chefs, Matt McGuire, Gerard Craft, and Jimmy Fiala, enthusiastically agreed to expound on how pecans are featured in their menus; thank you for bringing so much energy and jazz to our local food scene. We love and appreciate you.

We are extremely fortunate to be published by Rizzoli, and are deeply grateful to our cookbook editor, Jono Jarrett, and publisher, Charles Miers. Our editorial consultants, copy editor Sharon Silva, proofreader Eve Lynch, and indexer Ken DellaPenta, all helped put the final polish on this fascinating book.

Our families, now very familiar with the book creation process, continue to share their love, patience, and time, as well as encouragement and enthusiasm. To Barbara's children, Derek, Jamie, Christina, Justin, and Kelly, and grandchildren, Lillian, Jax, and Ladd—thank you for your love and support. To Betsy's husband, Sam, thanks for changing your allegiance to the food du jour and loving everything that appears on the table. To Betsy's family, Maddie, Nic, Clare, Andrew, Jane, Paul, Sam, Joe—you are the best people to cook for—and little Sammy and Thea—thanks for sharing your love of nuts at your tender age.

Christie Murphy and Jane Samuel, you'll recognize your hot mustard and carrot cake recipes; thanks for letting us include your treasured family recipes.

The Funsten and Pollnow families are part of Barbara's pecan heritage. Aunt Gee would roast pecans in butter at Christmastime, and the family would nibble them through the holiday season. Uncle Charles Pollnow continues to dazzle family and friends with his famous Sunday morning pecan waffles. His Sunday brunch door is always open.

To all of the people involved in the production and sharing of this book through conversations around their tables and via social media and beyond, please know our aprreciation is real and abiding.

FURTHER READING

Jackson, June. *In Praise of Pecans: Recipes & Recollections*. Houston: Bright Sky Press, 2007.

Manaster, Jane. *Pecans: The Story in a Nutshell*. Lubbock: Texas Tech University Press, 2008.

———. *The Pecan Tree*. Austin: University of Texas Press, 1994.

McWilliams, James. *The Pecan: A History of America's Native Nut*. Austin: University of Texas Press, 2013.

Purvis, Kathleen. *Pecans*. Chapel Hill: University of North Carolina Press, 2012.

Wells, Lenny. *Pecan: America's Native Nut Tree*. Tuscaloosa: University of Alabama Press, 2017.

———. *Southeastern Pecan Growers' Handbook*. Athens: University of Georgia Extension, 2017.

American Pecan Council

americanpecan.com

National Pecan Shellers Association

Ilovepecans.org